W9-BHY-415

and Publisher: Cynthia A. Zigmund
itor: Jonathan Malysiak
Editor: Trey Thoelcke
: Lucy Jenkins
ody Billert
zabeth Pitts

Underwood

earborn Trade Publishing
ssional Company

United States of America

7 6 5 4 3 2 1

gress Cataloging-in-Publication Data

n, 1941-
corporate IQ? : how the smartest companies learn, transform, and
erwood.

ex.
8573-4
planning. 2. Organizational learning. 3. Organizational change.
I. Title: Corporate IQ.   II. Title.
3   2004

2004009569

WHAT'S

CORPOR

HOW THE SMART
LEARN · TRANS

JIM UND

Dearb
Trade Pub
A **Kaplan Professio**

Vice Presiden
Acquisitions
Senior Proje
Interior Desi
Cover Design
Typesetting:

Published by
A Kaplan Pro

Printed in th

04 05 06 10 9

Library of C

Underwood,
  What's yo
lead / Jim U
    p.   cm.
  Includes i
  ISBN 0-79
  1. Strategi
4. Leadershi
  HD30.28.U
  658—dc22

Dearborn Tr
promotions,
Sales Depart
trade@dearl
Drive, Suite

To Harvey the Golden Retriever
More valuable than gold is a faithful companion.
October 1990–March 2004

Jim Underwood in this book has expanded the reaches of the practical, traditional methods of strategic analysis. His concepts were developed from proven research methodologies, practical business experiences, and, perhaps of most importance, from Underwood's leading hundreds of students through applications of strategic, analytical methodologies to real world situations. I recently had the good fortune to experience the application of Underwood's method as one of his graduate students. Moreover, having spent my career as an attorney, business executive (including chief executive officer of a large publicly traded company and a director of other publicly traded companies), and investor, I have the experience to evaluate the usefulness of this book outside of the academic environment. Needless to say, I find that it works well in all of these arenas.

First, the book offers a great tool to use in an academic environment. Students can easily follow and learn from the methodical step-by-step analysis. And the application of these steps can be visualized easily through the vivid, illustrative case examples. Different from many other books filling the idle space for this genre, this book simultaneously connects the student with the firm and with the environment within which the firm competes. As students have been accustomed to being graded, evaluated, and critiqued, the book serves as a transition for them (applying the same "how did I do?" thinking) to scoring, critiquing, and comparing firms within an industry.

Second, the book extends and improves upon traditional strategic thinking, providing a concrete, quantifiable method to rank companies within industries. Underwood has coined the phrase *Corporate IQ* to measure the degree to which a firm is prepared to operate within and meet the challenges emanating from its external environment. If the firm is prepared, it is generally in strategic balance and has a high IQ; if not, it will have a low IQ, indicating that remedial action must be taken for the firm to maximize its profit opportunities.

By focusing on profit opportunities, this book also becomes a book for investors. Smart investing for the long run involves betting on the best horse in a particular race. While I am sure that Underwood did not intend this book as an investment tool, one of my personal experiences convinces me that it should be so regarded.

Having served as a board member in Energy Service Company, an off-shore drilling contractor, for almost 20 years, I thought I had considered, or had at least been exposed, to most of the issues facing this firm, and I had my own, somewhat biased evaluation of the firm. Then came a study of the Underwood methodologies. It was revealing. Leading an Underwood student team through his methodical analysis provided me with new insights. Actually these insights pleasantly surprised me by showing me that the firm is in strategic balance and, as such, prepared to meet its competition and maximize profits in its industry. After giving these insights much thought, I decided to make a million dollar investment in Energy Service, which I hardly expected to make when I first began the Underwood course of study. While, as I said, I do not believe Underwood intended this result, my experience highlights why this book should be included in libraries for business academics, business executives, and investors looking to glean keen insights for their long-term investment decisions.

This book will set the industry standard for strategic thinking, and, hopefully, will give me an opportunity to report on the success of my particular investment in future editions. In any event, it has certainly provided me with the tools and methodologies for making business decisions and for analyzing corporate enterprises by keeping the focus on matching the internal capabilities of the firm with the external environment within which it operates.

Gerald W. Haddock,
Former CEO, president, and COO of Crescent Real Estate Equities
Director of Energy Service Company
Former general counsel of the Texas Rangers baseball club

WHERE'S THE BEEF?

Many people still remember that now famous line from the Wendy's television commercial: "Where's the beef?" When I heard about the ad, I was in a queue for a ski lift and the guy behind me blurted out, "Where's the beef?"

When I finally saw the commercial, I realized why they were laughing. The scene opened with a short, elderly woman holding an open hamburger on her hand. In the center of the open bun was a scrawny little beef patty about the size of a silver dollar. The large-sized bun made it appear even smaller. All of a sudden, in a raspy, horribly irritating voice, the little old lady looks down at the beef patty and asks, "Where's the beef?"

Where's the beef? has become a powerful communication phrase. When someone uses it, you immediately know what the speaker means. It has taken on a broad meaning from an applications standpoint and refers to the deficiencies of an idea or a product. It is a question that business managers need to learn to ask.

If you are the manager of an organization, it just makes sense that your primary business objective is to maximize profit. That is why *Where's the beef?* may be so important to you. You will discover, if you are insightful enough to ask that famous question, something important about many of your management practices.

Let me put it this way. A lot of business theories and practices do not hold up well when it comes to *Where's the beef?* In fact, a lot of those practices contribute more to organizational losses than to profits. That's why, "Where's the beef?" is such an important question for you to ask.

PERFORMANCE ISSUES AT MAINLINE MANUFACTURING

As a university professor, I expect a lot from my graduate students. At the completion of their MBA program, the students must go through a "capstone" class that synthesizes all of their learning into one experience. In the case of my students, they are required to consult for the senior executives of the some of the world's largest companies.

Recently, as one of those graduate teams was visiting with the senior division president of a global company, the executive asked what I thought of the *hoshin* strategic planning process. The executive seemed to glow with enthusiasm as we discussed the process, and he explained how they used it as their primary planning model.

I'm going to call the company "Mainline Manufacturing" to protect the guilty. Let me tell you a little about Mainline. Mainline is one of those companies that have been around for about 100 years. Their tenure and size gives them immediate worldwide name recognition. Like almost all 100-year companies, Mainline has been through its ups and downs. The executive explained how the firm had been through one of those periods of sustained losses but had gotten back on the right track and was again profitable.

With that in mind, let me paint a more detailed picture of the circumstances of this meeting. The graduate students had just completed a presentation of their analysis of the company. They had carefully detailed the statistical validity of their recommendations. They went to great lengths to explain the existing corporate deficiencies and why each one, if not corrected, would significantly impact future profit. They even cited the 1,000 studies that had been done over a 30-year period that supported the validity of their recommendations. Here is what they found.

- The firm's marketing lacked the aggressiveness required for success in the emerging environment.
- The firm's innovation and creation of new products was insufficient for the emerging environment.
- The firm's employees felt that management placed little value on them (a real performance killer).

- The leadership of the firm was controlling and risk averse, a real profit killer for this organization, considering the nature of the emerging environment.
- The firm's strategic planning process was not designed effectively for the emerging environment. It required extremely high levels of predictability for success, and the firm's emerging environment would clearly be highly unpredictable.

Keep in mind, my graduate students have been accurately predicting the performance of their *Fortune* 500 clients for the past 12 years. In the case of a number of privately held companies, they accurately predicted bankruptcy.

There is a reason why my students are successful in predicting the performance of companies. There is real beef behind their analyses and recommendations. Extremely reliable statistical relationships underlie everything that the students do. What would be surprising would be if they were wrong. Assuming that the input data gathered by my students is correct, the statistical correlation should hold true. There's the beef!

Let me explain what I am talking about. I visited with the executive for some time about the firm's strategy process. To be honest, I was not that familiar with *hoshin*. What I have learned in my research in the field of corporate strategy is that there are probably 500 different strategy approaches. What I have also discovered is that they are all similar, if not almost identical.

I discovered that *hoshin* is no different. It's a combination of BHAG's (Big Hairy Audacious Goals), an interim strategy adjustment process, and the traditional strategic planning approach (plus a total quality management component). It's a nice idea but not really much different from many other approaches.

The executive went on to explain that a nationally known author and consultant had worked with Mainline over the past few years and had led them to the *hoshin* model. Let's ask the question: where's the beef? In this situation, we have two strategic approaches. On one hand, no statistical data supports the use of the *hoshin* strategic planning and profit—none. On the other hand, the students' recommendations were based on decades of quality research. Statistical data backed up the relationship between their recommendations and future profit. There's the beef!

My point is that it makes little sense to be tied to a strategic approach with no relationship with organizational profitability when you have an option of using one that does. That is why it is so important for senior executives to be willing to ask, "Where's the beef?" In the case of Mainline Manufacturing, the "beef" wasn't there with *hoshin*. In the case of my students' work, it was there. The research validated the power of their recommendations.

THE RESEARCH STUDY

The study behind this book is founded on a much larger body of research. For the past 30 years, H. Igor Ansoff and his associates have been conducting studies on the topic of organizational performance. Over those 30 years, over 1,200 studies have been completed in countries around the world, in almost every major industry group. The outcomes of those studies have been phenomenally consistent. Across the board, companies that "match" their environment significantly outperform those that do not.

In designing the research study for *What's Your Corporate IQ?*, I was immediately faced with a major problem. To compute a company's IQ, I had to get internal access. Rather than being able to select a target group of companies and study them from the outside, I had to go with the companies that would give me access. In each case, I had to be sure that the internal source of information was dependable.

The research instrument measured two things. First, it measured what I call the competitor index, which describes the nature of a company's competitive segment on a scale of one to five. Second, it measured 17 different aspects of the company on a scale of one to five. Then, each of the 17 aspects was scored based on how close to the competitive index it was. The company could earn up to 10 points for each of the 17 aspects. Therefore, the highest Corporate IQ a company could have is 170.

Here is the raw data that I gathered.

Each organization completed the Corporate IQ assessment questionnaire. In most cases, I tried to get at least ten respondents to fill out the questionnaires. The target respondent was a midmanagement employee (versus a senior executive). Some might question the limiting the survey distribution to those in middle management roles. Our experience has been that the senior executives generally have limitations when it comes to understanding how their own organizations function. Accuracy is important, and we generally get the most accurate input from middle managers. Most of the companies were publicly traded, international organizations. A few were privately held.

Once the Corporate IQ of each company was determined, each was ranked based on its profit ranking (decile ranking) within its competitive

	CIQ	Rank
Mortgage	157	2
Entertainment	140	3
Retail Electrics	146	1
Telecommunications	40	10
Transportation	155	1
Consumer	167	1
Training	58	10
Investments	152	1
Technology-Medical	120	2
Bank	154	1
Bank	119	2
Mortgage	145	2
Industrial Products	134	2
Telecom-Corporate	160	2
Tech Manufactoring	95	6

segment. For example, you will note that the first mortgage company listed ranked in the top 20 percent of its segment. The company listed last, a technology manufacturer, ranked in the bottom 40 percent of its segment. A 1 ranking indicates a company in the top 10 percent; a 10 ranking indicates the company was in the bottom 10 percent of all companies.

The statistics were extremely encouraging. (See Appendix A.) The research revealed that the higher the Corporate IQ, the higher the ranking in its industry segment. The lower the Corporate IQ, the lower the ranking. This confirmed something that I have personally observed in hundreds of studies over the past 12 years: the original Ansoff model is highly predictive of organizational performance.

As I did additional research over the years, I discovered that a number of key issues needed to be added to Ansoff's original work. One of the most important, value of subordinates, is becoming even more important in today's highly competitive world. I have been fortunate to get an inside look at some of the world's most profitable and dynamic companies. Without fail, the exceptional companies place an extremely high value on subordinates.

In addition to the statistical backing, an additional bit of information is extremely encouraging. There has only been one instance of a high-scoring company that had problems, or failed. That company, Enron, was one I featured in a previous book. Fraud is a difficult issue to uncover. One of the real ironies of the Enron situation was that the executives who perpetrated the fraud did not need to involve the company in such acts to be successful. Regardless of any after-the-fact analysis, the company was well positioned to have a long, profitable life.

Another reality of the studies I've been involved in relates to low IQ companies. I've never seen a low Corporate IQ company that was doing well. From a research standpoint, the inferences we can make based on the Corporate IQ approach are quite encouraging. It is becoming apparent that it simply works.

One of the reasons that business research has gotten a bad name in some cases is an overreliance on researcher analysis, especially the use of simple averages from which conclusions are drawn and books are written. Even in academia, we seem to be enamored with the process of making deep statements about performance based only on observation and a few simple averages. As a number of people have pointed out, most great companies have a building, bathrooms, and a copy machine. That does not, however, correlate to profitability. Yet most of us in the business as well as the academic world seem blindly tied to the concepts of focus (mission, core competencies), best practices, benchmarking, and numerous other approaches. Yet, no facts support relating such practices to profitability.

That is why I am excited about the output of the research that surrounds *What's Your Corporate IQ?* It might be said that what is happening is the "mapping of corporate DNA." It is exciting to think about the possibility that the underlying drivers of corporate sustainability and profit are in the process of being identified. That's what the statistics are pointing toward. If that is true, and I hope it is, we are embarking on a new and powerful way of corporate governance, one in which fads are discounted and where we focus on the basics of sustainability and performance. There's the beef!

THE TEN SMARTEST COMPANIES IN AMERICA

As you will discover in the following chapters, Corporate IQ measures 17 areas of the firm. Basically, the Corporate IQ assessment provides a somewhat in-depth look at how the company does business, from its strategy and leadership to its corporate character and ethical standards. The key to Corporate IQ is that it provides an insider's view of the firm. That is why it is such a powerful diagnostic.

In conducting the early research about the smartest companies, I spent a number of months looking at different companies. My objective was to evaluate externally as many companies as possible to determine which ones had a chance of making the list. Then I began contacting different companies and asking for internally generated information. The first thing I asked was that a team of people go through the Corporate IQ assessment exercise. Once that was done, I selected the top ten companies for the list.

It should be pointed out that a few companies were not willing to give me access. Yahoo!, Inc., for example, was unwilling to participate. The same is true for Whole Foods, FedEx, and a number of others that passed my preliminary analysis. As an author, I am keenly aware that smart companies are also really busy companies, so I understand when a firm chooses not to participate. I did attempt to get access to all of those companies that passed the external assessment phase of my research.

Once the list of ten companies was determined, I then asked for access to the internal workings of the firm. Each firm's history was important as well. All of the research was organized around the 17 areas of the assessment. I looked for stories that illustrated what "smart companies" are all about. Finally, I asked for interviews with the senior executives of the firm. I usually find that smart companies are led by smart leaders. You will observe that I place a lot of value on leaders who manage both today and tomorrow well. With that in mind, I wanted to get some powerful quotes that illustrated the philosophies that those smart leaders held.

In the end, I think you will be convinced, as I am, that smart companies are different from their counterparts. They are managed with the future in mind. They do not mind taking a quarterly hit to their financial performance if it involves the long-term success of the firm. You will also note that all of the smart companies value their people. It's not just lip service; they live it. That may be why so many people seem to want to work for these smart companies.

I will also confess in advance that I have little sympathy for people and companies who blindly follow fads. A bestselling management book is a bestselling management book, but no more. Police officers stay alive on the streets because they quickly learn that they cannot trust anyone. The same is true of many management approaches. Don't trust anyone or any philosophy of management without testing it. Make sure it is worthy of your trust. If it doesn't work, reject it. In the end, you are betting your career and possibly your company on such a philosophy. Invest wisely and you will win.

Wisdom is the ability to see afar,
the distant result of this day's deeds.

SOCRATES

1

WHY COMPANIES WIN

Your Corporate IQ is extremely important if you happen to be a senior manager with an organization—or aspire to be one. I would like to start this book by answering the most obvious question of all: what is Corporate IQ?

Corporate IQ is a computation that involves three broad areas of the firm: strategy, organization, and character. Strategy deals with the firm's aggressiveness, organization deals with the firm's ability to adapt, and character deals with the firm's ability to sustain the first two. All three areas combined reveal just how capable the firm is of competing in the specific competitive segment it faces. That is why there is such a strong correlation between a firm's Corporate IQ and its industry ranking.

Let me begin by explaining that the firm's character, which involves ethics, value of subordinates, etc., is the *only* area where best practices and benchmark comparisons can be utilized. When it comes to the firm's strategy (marketing and innovation), there are no "best practices." The best strategy is one that fits its particular context well. The same is true for the firm's organization. There is no such thing as a "best in class" culture or structure. There is, however, an appropriate culture and structure (plus a lot of other corporate attributes) for each competitive context.

I would like to repeat what I just said, because it is radically different from what you probably have seen in the last 100 business books you have read. In fact, it is radically different from anything you might have read in the last 100 years. Organizations must have high standards of character, but the ability of the firm to match its strategies and organization with its competitive context determines whether or not it survives, thrives, or dies. It's that simple. Regrettably, there is no simple formula for success.

I once pursued a graduate degree in theology. One of the first courses I took was one called prolegomena. The word *prolegomena* literally means "that which goes before." The course dealt with the assumptions we make. In philosophy and theology, the assumptions you start with determine the outcome of your study. In philosophy, for example, the relativist, of necessity, concludes that there is no truth.

In the case of corporate management and strategy, prolegomena is critically important. Suppositions have an important impact on how you manage. More importantly, they directly impact the Corporate IQ of an organization. With that in mind, I will spend the first few chapters talking about the prolegomena of management philosophy. If you start out your management day assuming that the future will be a simple repetition of the past, you as well as your organization are destined to fail.

The assumptions that underlie corporate mission, core competencies, total quality management, excellence, and numerous other ideas have such built-in problems. That is why your ability to manage your organization's Corporate IQ is so important. It's all about being smart—aggressive, adaptive, with high levels of corporate character. Unlike a lot of the theories in the last 100 books you have read, Corporate IQ has facts to support it. Now I would like to begin introducing you to the idea of "smart companies."

The interest in so-called 100-year companies has tweaked the imagination of business leaders over the past few years, and rightly so. Most of the books on the topic seem to take what I call an "excellence" approach. In other words, the author tries to identify what "excellent" companies do.

There is one thing you must understand as you begin your reading of this book. There are three types of companies.

1. Companies that have lasted for 100 years
2. Companies that are designed to last for 100 years
3. Companies that will not survive for 100 years

One more thing is important to understand as you look at that list. The companies that meet criteria #2 (designed to last for 100 years) will generally have ROIs (return on investment) of 20 percent higher on a consistent basis than #1 and #3. That may be the most important aspect of this book. Further, understanding #2 and how to create a company designed to last for over 100 years is what this book is all about. Now let's take another look at the different types of companies.

You may think that there is little difference between the first two (we have little interest in the third for obvious reasons), but there is a world of difference between them. In some cases, it is clear that companies have somewhat "accidentally" lasted 100 years. In still others, there are companies that haven't yet been around for 100 years but will someday. While there is a lot of interest in companies that have lasted for 100 years and a number of books have been written on the subject, what is more important is the underlying truth that relates to why companies last 100 years.

Let me explain. The pharmaceutical called aspirin has been around for over 100 years. The benefits of aspirin continue to emerge. Aspirin is a product that has a sustainable demand of over 100 years. It would stand to reason that the first company to produce aspirin should still be on the world scene after 100 years. That's why I say that some companies last 100 years.

At the same time, if you were to find one of those 100-year companies that did not have a product like aspirin, with a long-term, sustainable demand, it would be an entirely different matter. What you would have in that case is a company that understood the difference between surviving with a sustainable product and a company that understood how to survive by continually reinventing itself and its products. See the difference? That's why some of the recent books on sustainability or so-called "100-year companies" may be misleading.

In many cases, the authors of such works will tell you that, if you do what these "excellent" companies do, your organization can be successful as well. As business managers, we tend to like such prescriptive ideas, because they are usually somewhat simplistic and understandable. After all, if I just had to do six things to be successful, that idea would be appealing.

One of the challenges of making such claims has to do with variables. Every researcher understands the problem of variables. We may discover, for example, that if we double the number of salespeople, our sales will go up. At the same time, that apparent correlation may lose credibility if we discover that we lowered the price of our product over the same time period. Research has to take into account all the variables that can impact your study.

When it comes to our 100-year companies, the same is true. Let's pretend that you could look at a company from two perspectives. On the surface, you might see that successful companies have tended to have dull, uninspiring leaders who place little value on innovation. However, if you looked behind the scenes, you might discover a company that had been founded 100 years earlier on a product that would be in demand for over 100 years. It is easy to see that if the demand for the product was over 100 years, corporate leadership would be somewhat irrelevant. What I just described is called a "demand cycle."

OIL WELLS: A GREAT ANALOGY

Did you know that oil wells come in numerous varieties with regard to how long they will be productive and how much oil they'll produce? In Russia, some of the old fields that were developed over 100 years ago are still producing a consistent amount of oil, as they have for all 100 years of their existence. They are still profitable due to the volume of oil the well can produce.

At the other end of the scale is an area called the Austin Chalk. Talk about heartbreak city, can you imagine drilling a well that flows 2,500 barrels of oil per day, only to drop to 1 to 3 barrels per day after a week or so? The fact is, when it comes to oil wells, some will bloom and quickly drop to almost nothing, while others will last for 100 years or more.

Companies are a bit like oil wells. Some tie into a "stream" that lasts for a century or so. Others tie into a stream that will last only a year or a few years. The stream or demand cycle, of course, is a critical issue in all of the research out there on the supposedly excellent companies.

WHEN THE WELL RUNS DRY

IBM was an innovator in mainframe computers. As long as the demand for mainframes was growing, IBM Corporation grew. When the demand for mainframes went into the tank, IBM almost ceased to exist.

Xerox was granted a patent on its xerography process in the 1960s. Xerox was one of those "excellent" companies, until the patent ran out around 1980. Xerox has never been able to return to its former level of greatness.

Joseph A. Schumpeter is the individual who best described the reality of such situations.[1] He coined the term *creative destruction* early in the last century. According to Schumpeter, companies and products are driven out of business by the creative efforts of entrepreneurs. Creative destruction has a number of variations.

> "Capitalism, then, is by nature a form or method of economic change and not only never is but never can be stationary."
>
> "[The history of American business is a] history of revolutions."
>   —Joseph A. Schumpeter, from *Capitalism, Socialism, and Democracy*[2]

Consider the sterile strip or Band-Aid that we put on a wound. It was a wonderful invention. The sterile strip still exists, although over the years it has undergone numerous modifications. Additionally, there have been attempts to develop substitutes for the sterile strip (thus illustrating the idea of creative destruction). Rather than replacing the sterile strip, substitutes, such as liquids that can be applied to wounds, have not replaced the strips. They are simply competitive products.

Another illustration of creative destruction is the current family of computer processors. We are moving toward a time in which opto-electronic applications will totally replace the current processor technologies. The creative destruction of that technology will be rapid and broad.

Some products (and consequently companies) are just like oil wells that last for 100 years. In others, creative destruction of the firm's products occurs every 50 years. In still others, creative destruction events may occur every 24 months. The issues are twofold.

1. How frequently do events of creative destruction impact a company's products?
2. Is the company prepared to anticipate and replace products creatively as they are driven to obsolescence?

Our exploration so far reveals the inadequacy of focusing upon historic "core competencies" as a basis for corporate strategy. Further, because environments are dynamic and not static, there is no such thing as "sustainable competitive advantage." Any advantage that a firm might have is momentary at best. The exceptional firm is dynamic. It is constantly becoming something different as opposed to focusing upon what it used to do well.

When creative destruction occurs, companies enter a time of decline. Of course, they hire consultants that tell them to "get back to basics" and

FIGURE 1.1   *Companies with 100-Year Product Demand Cycles*

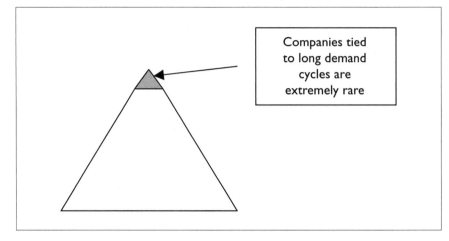

Companies tied
to long demand
cycles are
extremely rare

"focus on core businesses." However, the problem is that the basics have changed, as have the supposed core businesses.

What this means is that the key drivers of organizational sustainability or so-called "100-year companies" may be radically different than the literature currently indicates. Rather than being driven by six or so simplistic characteristics, the real truth regarding sustainability may have much more to do with the length of the demand curve of the company's products or, alternatively, the ability of the firm to anticipate and deal with events of creative destruction.

It is important to remember that creative destruction and complexity are one and the same. If two people are describing a pencil that occupies the same physical space and is identical in every way, we conclude that it is one pencil, not two (the "identity of the indiscernible" for philosophy fans). Creative destruction, in the eyes of the economist, is the process of one product being substituted by another due to competitor creativity. The complex systems management theorist would describe that as the outworking of complexity, or environmental change. Either way, they're basically talking about the same thing. The operating world has changed. Companies with the luxury of effectively emulating some of those "100-year companies" are few and far between. As Figure 1.1 shows, only a few are tied to product families with such sustainability.

The graphic illustrates just how few companies have products that can last for 100 years. Studying such companies is of little value if your company is engaged with competition that creatively destroys its product offerings and re-creates them periodically. The real area of interest should be in those companies that are continually re-creating themselves and their products to thrive in an environment of change and uncertainty.

If we set aside the companies that are tied to long demand cycles and look only at them, we will find that they are generally characterized by the term *stability*. Stability-based strategy can only survive in a market sector that is, in fact, stable. Richard Foster and Sarah Kaplan, in their book *Creative Destruction,* explain that, with rare exceptions, companies are operating in environments of change. The driving forces of creative destruction are continually changing the rules of the game. The subtitle of Foster and Kaplan's book makes the point quite well:

> *"Why Companies That Are Built to Last Underperform the Market"*
> —Taken from the subtitle of *Creative Destruction,* by Richard Foster and Sarah Kaplan

As a consultant, I have conducted research on a number of the companies that have been cited as 100-year companies. In one case, I conducted an extensive diagnosis of the firm. I concluded that the firm was operating at 60 to 80 percent of its profit potential and would continue to do so unless it dropped some of it's "founding practices." The issues are often hidden to the casual observer. With that in mind, I would like to introduce you to Corporate IQ.

CORPORATE IQ

Foster and Kaplan got a lot of things right in their book. The process of creative destruction, or environmental change and complexity, has everything to do with the profit-effectiveness of a company. It is important to remember that the commonly understood idea of "100-year companies" is built around the few that happen to be competing in a product family sector characterized by stability.

It is important to note, however, that a few companies are not tied to such a long demand cycle yet continue to thrive. GE, for example, continues to thrive but is not tied to product families with 100-year demand cycles. GE's success is tied to the ability of the firm to adjust proactively to continued cycles of complexity or creative destruction over long periods of time.

FIGURE I.2 *Companies with 100-Year Product Demand Cycles*

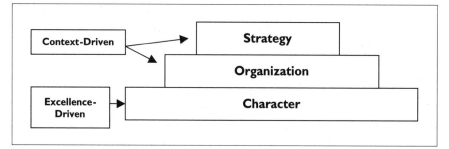

Companies that will last 100 years are a unique blend of context-driven attributes as well as having areas with only one standard: excellence. Strategy and organization must align with context, while corporate character must be unmovable and constant in all circumstances. Figure 1.2 illustrates those realities.

In developing the Corporate IQ scale for companies, I decided to use a scale of 1 to 170. My hypothesis was that low IQ companies would not perform well and high IQ companies would. The real breakthrough in the research was simply that I got it right. I studied 15 major companies, some top performers and some low performers, and across the board, the higher the IQ, the higher the ROI.

I based my work on that of H. Igor Ansoff, who first developed the idea of the role of management in equipping an organization with the complexity (and speed of change) to suit its competitive environment. Ansoff's work measured only 8 areas of the firm (I expanded his work to include 17 areas), but the results of the 1,000-plus studies conducted under his supervision were phenomenal. Companies that matched their context tended to have ROIs of 100 to 300 percent higher than their unmatched counterparts.

It is important to note that strategy and organization must match context. Context can and does change. At the same time, organizational character is measured against an unchangeable standard of excellence. The research conducted by Ansoff and his associates was monumental to say the least. They conducted over 1,000 studies in almost every country in the world, in almost every industry. No other strategic theory has such a body of material to support it.

In 1992, after studying under Dr. Ansoff during my doctoral program, I decided to continue the research around his model. The next decade provided additional insights into the validity of his concepts, especially when the model was expanded into the Corporate IQ model. During that time, I

FIGURE I.3   *The Seventeen Broad Areas of Corporate IQ*

STRATEGY	ORGANIZATION	CHARACTER
Marketing	CEO attributes	Values
Innovation	Managers	Ethics
Product-technology	Culture	Value of people
Product portfolio	Formal structure	Excellence rating
	Quality and process	
	Corporate strategy	
	Attitude toward change	
	Internal technology applications	

was able to study numerous global competitors, most of them Fortune 500 firms. Additionally, I worked with hundreds of CEOs at smaller companies. The results were overwhelming. I have never found a low IQ firm that was performing in the upper 50th percentile of its industry segment. The converse is true. I have never found a high IQ firm that was performing in the lower 50th percentile of its segment.

Not only have I found that the model accurately predicts future organizational profits, it further predicts corporate crisis, including bankruptcy. In the case of some of those 100-year companies that have been featured in the books, I have also found that many are operating well below their optimum level of performance. The reason is simply that the firm's leadership has chosen to stick with a strategy of stability instead of being open to adapting to environmental opportunity.

Corporate IQ focuses on three broad areas of the company: strategy, organization, and character. The failure to match any aspect of the first two with the organization's competitive context will result in diminished profit. The failure to match the character standard will also result in decreased profit versus what the firm could have achieved.

EDS

To better understand Corporate IQ, it might be beneficial to take a look at a number of different companies. The first we will consider is EDS. EDS is a company that has been through a number of drastic changes in its competitive environment.

Under the leadership of Les Abersol, the company built a massive, unresponsive bureaucracy. The company's strategy suffered due to the company's lack of focus on being a strategic first mover, and the culture of the firm became a risk-averse profile. When Abersol left the firm, the external environment had become highly competitive and was characterized by high rates of change and complexity. His leadership had created a bureaucratic organization that was unable to deal with the level of continual creative destruction that was occurring in the firm's various competitive segments. At the time of Abersol's departure, the firm's strategies were problematic at best, the firm's organization was equally flawed, but the firm's character remained intact. Enter Richard Brown.

Brown brought in an era of executive intimidation. In many ways, his era destroyed what was left: the firm's character. No longer were individuals valued or appreciated. The only thing that mattered was "making the quarterly numbers." The intimidation factor that Brown brought to the company did enhance the level of strategic aggressiveness for a time, but the ability of the organization to support high levels of creativity and risk taking was summarily destroyed. Additionally, the character of the firm was destroyed. People no longer viewed their jobs as important and began to act accordingly.

When we look at the decline of EDS, what we see is a systematic destruction of the ability of the firm to deal with environmental uncertainty. The firm's strategy lacked appropriate aggressiveness, the organization was no longer able to support entrepreneurial efforts, and the character of the organization was destroyed.

AMERICAN AIRLINES

One of the things that Bob Crandall brought to the airline industry was his ability to manage the numbers. As American left the regulated environment to enter the unregulated environment, Crandall supervised the development of systems that would allow him to manage the entire airline "by the numbers." The result was what might be called "acceptable neglect." Customer service standards, previously exceptionally high, were modified in the interest of profit in the new competitive environment. The old AA culture of maximizing the customer experience was replaced by a numbers-driven approach of acceptable neglect. Analysts were able to compute the millions of dollars in savings that resulted from allowing customers to experience longer wait times on the phone. It all became a numbers game.

While the airline's strategies remained well suited for the environment or competitive context, the organization steadily became unable to support entrepreneurial behavior (a critical behavior for times of uncertainty). More importantly, the organization's character went from one that valued its people to one that had little regard for people. It was all about numbers.

Problem was, American had competitors that placed extremely high value on their customers and employees. More importantly, those competitors understood the critical competitive differences provided by such actions. As American's organization and character declined, its competitors got the message and began aggressive campaigns to create highly adaptive organizations and character that placed a high value on people and ethical behavior.

In April of 2003, American's unions were given an ultimatum that involved significant pay decreases if the company was to have a chance of avoiding bankruptcy. Just one day after the pilots, ground workers, and flight attendants narrowly approved the new contract agreement, the press revealed that the board of American had voted to spend millions to guarantee the retirement income plus future bonuses of the senior managers of American in the event of bankruptcy.

Unquestionably, the character of the organization was damaged. One of the key components of organizational character is trust. Intentional or not, what the board of American did was to confirm the lack of trust that existed among American's various labor groups.

Strategy, organization, and character: strategy and organization must fit the competitive environment, and character must be unquestionable if an organization is to succeed on a long-term basis. In environments of low levels of competitiveness, deficiencies (lower Corporate IQ) are less destructive than when competition and complexity is extremely high.

THE OTHER (AND A MOST IMPORTANT) VARIABLE: CONTEXT

I have alluded to the idea of context in a number of ways in this chapter. Creative destruction is all about context. Context has to do with the variables that are outside of the company. The creative, aggressive intervention of competitors into a firm's business segments usually changes the context in with the firm is operating. Again, when we talk about complexity and creative destruction, they are basically the same things. When it comes to managing a company, the forces of complexity and competition can be extremely difficult to comprehend, because companies are subject to both global

FIGURE 1.4   *Understanding the Global Competitive Context or Environment*

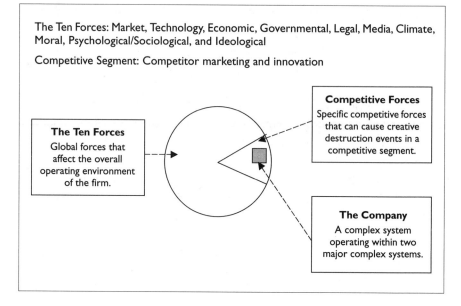

The Ten Forces: Market, Technology, Economic, Governmental, Legal, Media, Climate, Moral, Psychological/Sociological, and Ideological

Competitive Segment: Competitor marketing and innovation

The Ten Forces
Global forces that affect the overall operating environment of the firm.

Competitive Forces
Specific competitive forces that can cause creative destruction events in a competitive segment.

The Company
A complex system operating within two major complex systems.

forces as well as competitive forces. Consider Figure 1.4, which reveals those challenges.

John W. Sutherland suggested that companies are generally operating in one of four environments. In his exceptional book, *Strategic Renaissance,* Evan Dudik did a great job of summarizing Sutherland's idea.

1. Deterministic (highly predictable)
2. Moderately variable (mostly predictable)
3. Severely variable (generally unpredictable)
4. Indeterminate (totally unpredictable)

Dudik argues that strategy must be contingent, or based on, the predictability of the firm's context. We can see that Sutherland provides us a way of understanding context by framing it in terms of predictability. Notice that we can apply Sutherland's ideas in relation to both the global forces (the ten forces) as well as the competitive segment forces (marketing and innovation forces that specifically relate to our product portfolio). In that context, we can immediately see the impact of the 9/11 tragedy (ideological forces) on the airline business. At the same time, we can see that competitors' activities in the airline segment will have a direct impact on an airline company as well.

In using Corporate IQ, it's easy to pick winners and losers in a competitive segment. For example, even if United Airlines were able to make some of the basic changes in routes, airports, and aircraft to match those of Southwest, the firm would still not be competitive with their counterpart. They lack the organization and the character to execute any strategy that requires high levels of flexibility and aggressiveness.

One of the ironies in the United situation is the relationships between the unions and the corporation. The unions have been unable to give up their traditional adversarial approach in dealing with the corporation, even though the company is owned by the union membership. I would like to introduce you briefly to one of the smartest companies in America. Such smart companies will be discussed in depth in the second half of the book.

THE TOP TEN SMARTEST COMPANIES IN AMERICA

The screening of companies for my research initially included a fairly extensive list. It should be remembered that the Corporate IQ assessment requires internal access to the organization, not just to its senior management. In some cases, companies were eliminated due to low Corporate IQs. In others, a number of exceptional companies chose not to be considered. The final list of ten companies was compiled from those that scored quite high on the Corporate IQ assessment.

It is important to remember that Corporate IQ is a measure of a broad spectrum of corporate attributes. Rather than being based on a "best in class" approach, Corporate IQ assesses how well a company's strategies and organization are equipped for their emerging competitive context. That said, there is no such thing as "best practices," only a best practice for each different competitive context.

As I said, we begin by comparing a company's strategies and organization with its context. There is a third broad area that is assessed called "corporate character." In that area, it might be fair to say that there is only one acceptable standard. Because factors like corporate ethics are included in character, it makes sense that only one standard is acceptable.

The simple reality of Corporate IQ is that it measures the ability of a firm to behave competitively and stay in the "profit zone" in every aspect of its being. It includes marketing, innovation, CEO, leadership, culture, technology, and other areas that are critical to long-term success. In the area of character, the Corporate IQ assessment measures the various characteristics of the firm that have to do with sustainability. Companies with a high Corporate IQ will have appropriately aggressive strategies, highly adaptive organizations, and an internal character of the highest standard. They are winners simply because they are smarter than their counterparts.

In the next eight chapters, a short snippet of each company will be featured. The snippets are overviews of the companies and are designed to bring out a few of the things these companies do well. As you will see, the second half of the book is devoted to more extensive coverage of just why these smart companies are so exceptional.

DELL COMPUTER: ONE OF THE TEN SMARTEST COMPANIES IN AMERICA

When it comes to crazy competitive environments, Dell lives there. Although Dell avoids the high cost research and development projects that some competitors seem to enjoy, Dell is still able to be a first-to-market competitor. The reason for their success is the company's ability to deal with both complexity and speed in their competitive environment.

It is fair to say that employees are the key to managing knowledge, which is the basis of competitive success. Like other smart companies, Dell is clearly both customercentric and employeecentric. The result of those approaches is an organization that is highly aggressive when anticipating customer needs and is also highly adaptive when responding to competitive thrusts.

If you were to boil it all down to one simple principle, Dell's people and systems allow it to find the sweet spot in the customer adoption process. *Sweet spot* is a tennis term that describes the area of the racquet that produces the most power and speed. The sweet spot in the product diffusion curve is the point at which a technology becomes a certainty. With a lot of competing computer technologies hitting the market, Dell's ability to pick winners quickly makes them a really smart company.

CREATING A COMPANY THAT WILL LAST 100 YEARS

When it comes to creating a company that will last 100 years, there are two options. You can get really lucky and choose a segment in which your product will still be in demand in 100 years, or you can create a company that is capable of continually matching its competitive context with its strategy, organization, and character.

Keep in mind, I have never seen a company with a high corporate IQ that was threatened with extinction. Certainly a number of the exceptional companies have been in situations (like the airline industry) in which the entire industry has been impacted with unexpected, frame-breaking change. At the same time, what I continually see is that the high IQ companies will continue to out perform the low IQ companies and emerge from periods of extreme change as even better competitors. Usually, when such events occur, the low IQ competitors go out of business.

> *I have never found a high IQ company that was in trouble.*

When it comes to understanding leadership and why companies last 100 years, looking at some of the 100-year companies is not necessarily helpful. Once we segment out the ones that were tied to products with long demand cycles, we gain important insights. We should be studying the company that is *not* tied to a product family with a 100-year demand cycle. It is important to understand that the reason Southwest Airlines is doing well during the post–9/11 airline industry meltdown is related more to its strategy-organization-character profile than anything else.

Why are some companies a lot like the famous "Energizer bunny" in the television commercials? Why do some companies just keep on going, while others fade into oblivion? The answer to those questions is revealed in the research on Corporate IQ. Regrettably, long-term sustainability is all about strategy, organization, and character. I said "regrettably," because managing a complex system (a company) in a highly complex environment is not simple. Copying six best practices of excellence will not get you to first base, if your organization is deluged with the uncertainty of a highly complex environment.

But there is good news. If you are willing to challenge your current paradigm of strategy and management, it is possible to understand how to create one those high IQ organizations that will last 100 years. By the way, if you are willing to do that, not only will your company make a lot of money, but you'll also love working there. More importantly, so will your employees. Happiness is a choice, and so is success.

I started this chapter with a somewhat startling claim about "companies that are *designed* to last over 100 years." What I said was that those companies will consistently have ROIs that are 20 percent higher than the two other types of companies, the so-called 100-year companies with 100-year products and those that will clearly not survive for 100 years. As you conclude this chapter, it is important for you to understand that I am making that claim based on hard research. Simply put, companies with high Corporate IQs will consistently outperform their lower IQ counterparts to the tune of at least 20 percent.

2

WHY COMPANIES FAIL

Companies fail because they have a low Corporate IQ. That's a proven fact. Underlying Corporate IQ is the idea that the competitive environment is complex and may operate at varying levels of complexity as well as rate of change. Simply put, not-so-smart companies operate without regard to their competitive context. As you will discover, that is a death sentence for an organization.

If you look back in history, you will find that change has often been slow, and except for a few interruptions, it has also been quite steady. The reason for so much recent interest in Joseph Sumpeter's concept of "creative destruction" is that those interruptions have increased in frequency. In fact, we have moved from an environment in which disruptive events, or frame-breaking changes in the "rules of the game," would occur every few decades to a world in which they occur every few months.

Creative **D**estruction

Creative destruction is the result of scientific discovery, competitor innovation, or both. The end result is that products and processes that formerly satisfied purchasers' needs are no longer viewed as relevant by the most important player in the economic process: *The Customer.*

When it comes to customers, there is one company that has been able to establish a new standard in its industry. Barely 20 years old, Luxottica Retail (Lens Crafters, Watch Station, and Sunglass Hut) has become one of the top ten smartest companies in America.

LUXOTTICA RETAIL: ONE OF THE TEN SMARTEST COMPANIES IN AMERICA

When you took your last job, were you told that you could earn the opportunity to go on a "mission trip"? Chances are, you were not, unless you were applying at one of Luxottica Retail's companies: Sunglass Hut, Watch Station, or LensCrafters. Associates have the opportunity to compete to be one of the few people selected to go around the world each year as part of the company's "Gift of Sight" program.

As of 2004, over 3 million people around the world have received eye exams and/or glasses from one of Luxottica Retail's volunteer associates and doctors. In some cases, the recipients were able to see for the first time in their lives.

Luxottica Group Retail is an NYSE listed company (NYSE: LUX). The retail division began in the United States just 20 years ago. A group of executives wanted to create a company that valued its people and was focused on excellence. They chose the brand LensCrafters. One of the things that the Luxottica leadership has realized is that their worldwide charity projects change their people. By helping the less fortunate, their people become even more customer focused.

The result is a group of companies with the lowest employee turnover rate in their industries. It has also enjoyed a stellar 20 years of earnings and revenue growth.

In many ways, Luxottica Retail is driven by its employees. In one series of meetings, the Luxottica Retail leadership team was challenged to change the company's values to include "uncompromising integrity." It was not a case that the company did not already hold that value; it was a reflection of the employees' existing beliefs about the company. They felt it was important to emphasize the importance of uncompromising integrity in every associate's dealings with vendors, customers, and, of course, the recipients of the Gift of Sight program.

A philosophy within Luxottica Retail drives the idea of challenging every standard with a better one. It is prevalent at the top as well as the bottom

FIGURE 2.1   *In the 1800s and Early 1900s*

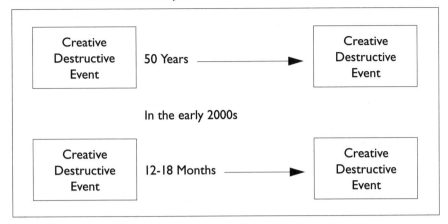

of the organization. Luxottica Retail is one of those smart companies that realizes that great strategy can only turn into profit when it is supported by a great organization that lives the highest ideals of corporate character.

Companies like Luxottica Retail will do extremely well regardless of the business they are in. They are people-focused organizations that deliver consistently high customer service. Some, unlike Luxottica Retail, lack the ability to deal with the chaotic changes that periodically hit almost every industry.

Think about it. In the 1930s, if you were in the radio manufacturing business, you didn't have a lot to worry about. Only in the 1940s did an event of potential creative destruction—television—begin to impact the business. If we look back at history, what we discover is that creative destruction events, or so-called "frame breaking change," used to occur rarely.

Between early 2001 and late 2002, the following events rocked the world:

- Terrorists reached a new low in the events of 9/11, which precipitated a worldwide recession.
- The Enron scandal and other ethics scandals rocked global stock markets.
- The Internet and technology bubble of the 1990s collapsed and investors had a hard landing.

As Figure 2.1 illustrates, in past centuries, companies often had a long time to adjust to change. A number of things happen when the creative efforts of competitors (or other forces, such as terrorists) precipitate a creative destruction event.

- The rules of the game change.
- The company's rules of engagement (must) change.

This leads us to the underlying issues related to why companies fail. Management philosophy over the past century has been, and continues to be, consumed with linear thinking or "sameness."

Here's what I mean. When was the last time you heard a new CEO take over a company and say, "We're going to divest ourselves of slow-growth, low-profit products and move to high-growth, high-profit segments regardless of where we have to go." Of course you haven't heard a new CEO say that. What you have heard is this: "We're going to refocus on our core business."

Allow me to translate this: "We're going back to what we used to do." Does that make any sense? It might, in some cases, but if the rules of the game have changed and the rules of engagement have changed, getting back to your "historic competencies" will only accelerate your losses. That simply makes no sense, yet we hear such comments almost weekly from new CEOs who are in exactly that situation.

Management, I often say, is all about philosophy. How you think is what you do. Whatever your management philosophy, that will drive your behavior. It's the philosophies behind most management theories that really explain business problems. When you get down to it, six ideas underlie management thinking as it has progressed to its current state. They are the following:

1. Equilibrium theory
2. Complex adaptive systems
3. Emergence
4. Excellence
5. Creative destruction
6. Complex dynamic systems

To understand how managers think and why companies fail, it is important to understand each of these approaches. I will confess in advance, some will seem a bit silly. At the same time, it is important to remember that best-selling books have been written about most of these ideas. Following is a brief explanation of each of these approaches to management and corporate strategy.

Equilibrium Theory

Equilibrium theory is a great economic theory. It's been around for a couple of centuries, and the entire idea of supply and demand came from it. Included in equilibrium theory is economist David Ricardo's idea of the "theory of comparative advantage." Ricardo concluded from his studies that each country had a unique set of attributes that meant that they were well suited for a specific group of industries. For example, some of the countries in the areas around Thailand and Laos were especially suited to grow rice. The climate was right, and cheap labor was available. Others would be at a disadvantage in competing with those countries. Thus, Thailand has a "comparative advantage" over its competitors when it comes to producing rice.

When the management theorists of the 20th century studied Ricardo's theory of competitive advantage, many jumped to the conclusion that Ricardo's ideas could be applied metaphorically to management theory. They advanced the idea that each company had a unique set of assets and attributes that gave them an advantage over others in a specific industry segment. The key, they hypothesized, was to keep the company "in the box." This is sometimes called a "focus" strategy. The idea is to operate where you have a competitive advantage and to avoid competing in segments where you are at a competitive disadvantage. To make sure that everyone in the company stayed in the box, the theorists developed the idea of the mission. The purpose of the mission was to make sure that the company focused on its unique area of competitive advantage. In other words, the company had to stay in the box to be successful.

The purpose of the Mission Statement is to keep the company "in the box," so that it will not succumb to temptation to compete where others have competitive advantage.

Over the years, it became obvious to many in the management field that adapting the idea of the "theory of comparative advantage" made little sense. Further, there really do not appear to be things like "core competencies" and sustainable advantage. The competitive world is much too complex and changes much too frequently for that approach to managing a company to be logical. The reality of creative destruction renders any supposed advantage unsustainable.

In the 1990s, a number of those who rejected the idea of a linear world, as espoused by the equilibrium theory crowd, concluded that the world was much more complex than previously thought. So they decided to focus on the idea of nonlinear, or complex, systems thinking. There were two different thoughts (at that time) on complexity. One held to a "biological" view of the world, and the other took on what I call an "emergence" view of complexity.

Biological or Ecological Management

This group of people decided that the business world is metaphorically identical to nature (as they saw it). They decided that Charles Darwin's concept of evolution was an appropriate metaphor for the complex system called business. Behind the idea of biological management is the assumption that an invisible "force" of reality causes systems to behave in a certain way. Those who hold this idea of the invisible force suggest that, just as in nature, organizations mimic organisms by upward evolution. The "survival of the fittest" results in an upward spiral of increasing complexity and intelligence.

In the scientific world, Darwinism is difficult to support. Mutations, for example, never result in an increase in complexity. In fact, mutations always decrease the complexity of an organism. Charles Darwin himself recognized that there is no fossil record evidence to support the hypothesis that one species can become another.[1] (So much for the idea of kissing a frog that promises to become a prince.) Tragically, instead of adapting to changes in the environment, over 100 species cease to exist every year.[2]

At the same time, the idea of biological management makes little sense for the business manager. There is no empirical evidence to support the idea of "self organization" as hypothesized by those who support the concept.

Emergence

In 1957, Herbert Simon suggested that the human mind's ability to comprehend the complexity of a system was significantly limited when compared to the actual complexity of a system. Thus was the term *bounded rationality* was coined, meaning that the human mind cannot comprehend the numerous levels of complexity that exist in a system.

Two theorists in particular adapted Simon's idea and applied it to the business arena: Henry Minztberg[3] and Ralph Stacey.[4] Mintzberg and Stacey avoided the trap of biological management and chose to focus only on the idea of complexity and bounded rationality. Rather than assume a biological metaphor, Mintzberg and Stacey suggested that issues can only be managed after they have occurred. In other words, due to the mental overload caused by bounded rationality, any attempt to plan for the future is insufficient. The result of their thinking is that "emergence" is the proper philosophical paradigm. That is, "wait until something happens" is the best way to manage an organization.

Obviously, emergence is just one aspect of organizational governance and one way to make sure that the firm is prepared to deal with the surprises that come from complexity. In fact, the best companies are those that manage both the present emergent system as well as the future. It's simply a "both" situation. Smart companies and smart leaders understand that they must manage the future as well as the emergent discontinuities of the present.

Often, managers become uncomfortable with the idea of constant change. Research on change reveals that human beings generally do not like it. Many seek to accomplish only superficial change, while at the same time sticking with the firm's historic competencies. I call this approach the "excellence" approach.

Jim Collins and Jerry Porras make an excellent point about this approach.[5] It is possible to conclude that all excellent companies have at least one thing in common: a building. They have a lot more things in common: restrooms, doors, copy machines, etc. Their point is that descriptive statistics like the above may appear to shed light on why companies achieve sustainable performance, but in reality, they are not valid relationships. The problem is, people like them.

In fact, book publishers will tell you that if you can write a simple book about "best practices" or "excellence" with a list of five to seven keys, you may have a bestseller. You see, "excellence" infers that we can keep on focusing upon our historic competencies—that we can correct our corporate deficiencies without having to think about change.

I want you to think back a few pages. Remember the chart I drew that showed how often creative destruction events occurred in past centuries? Do you also remember the difference I pointed out in just the years 2001 and 2002? That's the problem with excellence. Not only does it allow the firm to stay in its old historic competencies rut, but it makes sure that you avoid meaningful change. Simply by looking at the realities of the frame-breaking changes of 2001 and 2002, it immediately becomes apparent that most companies have to think about being something entirely different on a more frequent basis.

That leads us to a new idea called "next practices." The concept that a firm needs to involve itself continually in creating the next practices for its industry segment makes a lot more sense than trying to copy something that someone else has done. After all, we usually have no basis in fact to support the copying of a practice.

This leads us to the fifth concept of business thinking. That concept, which I have previously introduced in this chapter, is called creative destruction.

Creative Destruction

In the first half of the 20th century, as the management field was in its infancy, an economist named Joseph A. Schumpeter made some astounding comments about equilibrium theory. He said that the idea had some merit, except that the periodic creativity of entrepreneurs brought about the destruction of the existing equilibrium and established an entirely new system of competition.[6] What he hypothesized is that the creative destruction of competitors changes the rules of the game. Again, when the rules of the game change, competitors must change their rules of engagement.

To recognize the reality of Schumpeter's ideas as they apply to business, we need only to look at the years 1900 to 2000. We can observe two things about that century. First, it was characterized by a number of frame-breaking shifts. Second, the frequency of frame breaking or creative destruction events accelerated each decade. By the end of the century, such events were rapid and filled with surprises.

If you doubt this, consider medicine, banking, pharmaceuticals, office products, retailing, learning, or almost any other product or activity at the beginning of the century. After 100 years, nothing was even remotely the same.

One of the reasons that we should pay a great deal of attention to the idea of creative destruction is simply that it is true. When we look at the history of businesses and industries, we see creative destruction events. Creative destruction destroys the existing system in favor of a new system of competition. The fact is, creative destruction is reality. The problem is, now

FIGURE 2.2   *The Ten Forces Model*

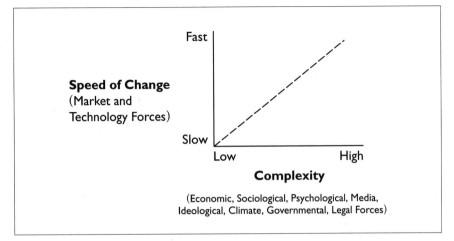

that we understand that it is reality, what can we do about it? How do we understand the new rules of the game, and how do we know what new rules of engagement our company should deploy?

Interesting isn't it? Of the first five ideas of how the world works, only one of those I've discussed has any validity when we look at the world in general. Global business enterprises have spent a great deal of time and money on management approaches that simply do not work. I'm going to address this issue at the end of the chapter, but first I'd like to discuss the last of the six ideas regarding how the business system works.

Complex Dynamic Systems

Earlier, I mentioned the work of H. Igor Ansoff. I was fortunate in my business studies to have the opportunity to study under Ansoff, the recognized "father of strategic management" and, in my opinion, the top strategist of the 20th century. It was Ansoff who introduced me to W.R. Ashby's requisite variety theorem. Ashby suggested that business systems involve two important dynamics: speed of change and complexity.[7] In subsequent research, I discovered a lot of support for his ideas. From that, I developed what I call the ten forces model and the concept of complex dynamic systems.

The ten forces are those that affect the global environment. They affect every aspect of the business community. In the case of a company, additional issues must be considered: I call these areas the "competitive segment." In addition to the general effects of the ten forces, each competitive segment

FIGURE 2.3   *The Company, Its Competitive Segment, and the Global Environment*

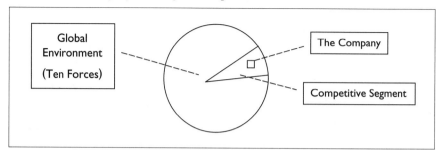

in which a firm operates is subject to the specific creative or competitive acts of other firms in that segment. As a result, the firm is a lot like a ship in a storm. Not only does the ship's captain have to deal with the effects of the storm, but the changing currents also impact the ship's path. To remain safe, a skipper must account for both factors. The same is true for a company. The CEO must ensure that the firm deals with the speed/complexity issues that relate to the general business environment and, at the same time, deal with the speed/complexity issues of the competitive segment.

Corporate leaders who fail to account for either the global environment or the creative competitive action of opponents will usually end up failing. The greater the degree of mismatch, or lack of strategic fit, the faster the company will fail or the more money it will lose.

My research into both the ten forces and the idea of competitive segments supports the idea of complex dynamic systems. Complex dynamic systems are an observable reality. That is not true of complex adaptive systems (Darwinism), emergence, or excellence. Equilibrium theory, when combined with creative destruction, makes a lot of sense. At the same time, when you combine equilibrium theory with creative destruction, you are really describing . . . you guessed it: complex dynamic systems.

Companies fail because their leaders fail to recognize the external reality of complex dynamic systems. As a result, they don't design an organization that can operate at the speed or level of complexity that the firm will face in both the global environment and the competitive segment. Let's state this in a more positive way: firms that are in strategic fit with their global environment and their competitive segment will deliver creative destruction to their competitors. Simply put, smart companies, those in strategic fit, are consistent winners. Companies lose because they fail to fit the global environment or segment into which they are moving.

Ram Charan and Jerry Useem's 2002 article in *Fortune* concluded that there are ten reasons that lead companies to fail.[8]

1. Slave to Wall Street
2. See no evil
3. Overdosing on risk
4. Dysfunctional board
5. Softened by success
6. Strategy du jour
7. Acquisition lust
8. Fearing the boss
9. Dangerous culture
10. Death spiral

Generally speaking, Charan and Useem got it right. At the same time, rather than calling these the "ten big mistakes" that leaders and companies make, it might be better to classify them as "ten symptoms." All of these mistakes are rooted in leaders' failure to understand the demands of the competitive environment and what it will take to succeed in that environment.

Take a look at some of these issues and the problem becomes clear. "Fearing the boss" is one example. The research shows that high-complexity environments (those with high levels of uncertainty) require high levels of trust, integrity, and empowerment. My research has shown that highly controlling management severely impacts corporate profit in such uncertainty. Chasing the "fad du jour" is another example that the firm's leaders have absolutely no idea what they should be doing. Take a look at what the average firm has endured in just the last ten years.

- A total quality management initiative
- A process reengineering initiative
- Downsizing
- Seven Habits training
- Open book management
- Change seminars
- Built-to-Last/Good-to-Great training (Collins and Porras/Collins)
- Six Sigma
- Execution seminars and/or training

Like the little old lady in the now famous Wendy's commercial of years ago, I have a question: Where's the beef? In other words, where are the statistical links between some of these teachings and profit?

I'll let you answer that question for yourself. Keep in mind, each of these ideas has a lot of merit. I routinely prescribe process reengineering to clients that need shorter cycle times to serve their customers more effectively. Note what I am saying.

- Understand the problem.
- Use the appropriate tool to correct the problem.

I would like to suggest that Dr. Seuss got it right. If you have no idea what the real problem is, you probably have no idea of how to correct an organization's profit situation.

> When you know where things are out of whack . . .
> then you know how to get things back in whack.
> —Dr. Seuss

Most people never stop to figure out what is out of whack. In fact, the very idea of figuring out what's out of whack is foreign to most business managers. Let's take an honest look at how most companies' CEOs deal with bad quarterly profits. You are correct: they eliminate people. Did those people cause the problem? No! Did they fail to take appropriate action when they recognized that something was not right? No! In fact, the very people who got downsized are often the same people who were screaming at the top of their lungs, trying to get senior management's attention about the very problem that caused the decreased earnings.

Sydney Finkelstein, in his book *Why Smart Executives Fail,* lists "Seven Habits of Spectacularly Unsuccessful Executives."[9]

1. They see themselves and their companies as dominating the environment.
2. They identify so completely with the company that no clear boundary exists between their personal interests and their corporation's interests.
3. They think they have all the answers.

One of the joys of my life is when I see someone grasp something that can really benefit them. As I lead you to an in-depth look at Corporate IQ in a few chapters, I hope that you will be patient as I attempt to build the foundations of the concept. The outcome is a radical way of looking at the role of the manager and how they can truly make a long-term difference in an organization. If you want to know how to maximize profit and create one of those 100-year companies, your patience will pay off. The journey to that understanding begins with the three rules of strategy in the next chapter.

3

THE THREE RULES OF LEADERSHIP AND STRATEGY

Smart companies create sustainable success, and stupid companies do not. That's what Corporate IQ is all about. When you boil it down, smart companies are simply servants. They serve their customers, shareholders, and employees. Smart companies differ from their not-so-smart competitors in a number of ways.

- Smart companies are living, growing organizations. It's important that you do not mistake this statement as support for a "biological" model.
- High IQ companies (leaders) understand that corporate ego trips end in disaster. They have corporate humility and, as a result, understand just how critical the customer, the people who serve the customer (employees), and those who risk their money (the shareholders) really are.
- High IQ companies last a long time. Their less than smart counterparts do not.
- Corporate IQ is sustained by corporate culture and by CEOs who understand their roles as enablers.

Research is revealing that underneath the success of every organization is a complex set of attributes that either drive or destroy success. I have combined all of that research into a composite whole, called Corporate IQ.

What I have discovered is simply that companies with high Corporate IQ will consistently outperform those with low Corporate IQ.[1]

Some corporate founders were wise enough to ingrain a high Corporate IQ into their firms. Over the years, those companies' boards and their CEOs have been successful in maintaining the firms' Corporate IQ. Generally, those who create high IQ companies have a very deep understanding of the drivers of corporate performance and sustainability. It takes only one generation of board or CEO to destroy a firm's Corporate IQ.

What does a high Corporate IQ firm look like? They usually have hundreds of applicants for every job. They often earn "best to work for" recognition. They often have an unusual ability to anticipate customer needs (versus staying close to the customer). They also have a preoccupation with excellence that permeates every aspect of their company. They are usually the first to discover the future and the first to adapt to where the future will take them. They care little about historic core competencies or competitive advantage, instead focusing on what the firm needs to become to sustain success. Rather than falling into the trap of focusing on any "core business," they allocate assets according to future attractiveness. They are not married to any business or any product. They are committed to maximizing the future prospects of their company, its employees, its shareholders, and its customers.

Simply put, companies with a high Corporate IQ are committed to maximizing both today and tomorrow. And they make sure they never get off track. One of the companies that maximizes today as well as tomorrow is Costco Wholesale, one of the top ten smartest companies in America.

COSTCO WHOLESALE: ONE OF THE TEN SMARTEST COMPANIES IN AMERICA

Can you imagine a company whose legal and real estate staffs diligently review local construction laws, then makes sure that the firm exceeds all the local requirements? Can you imagine an organization that argues with some of the Wall Street analysts when they call for lower employee benefits and salaries, trying to explain to them that taking care of their employees is the right thing to do for the long-term benefit of its stock price? You do not have to imagine such a scenario. All you have to do is take a look at Costco.

One would expect this much smaller competitor of Sam's Wholesale (Wal-Mart's warehouse club) to struggle against its much larger competitor.

Actually, the reverse is true. Costco consistently gets better results than its larger competitor.

"It's all about our people," said executive vice president Richard Galanti. He explained that Costco utilizes an aggressive strategic approach that involves a consistent (and, I might add, fairly low) profit margin on products and combines that with seamless processes. Galanti believes that Wall Street often places too much emphasis on short-term profits, thereby failing to appreciate that having higher wages and benefits leads to higher quality employees; lower employee turnover; greater productivity; and, ultimately, higher long-term profitability. He believes that Costco is a rapid response machine that is totally dependent upon its people. "That's why we try to make sure we hire and keep the best," he said.

While competitors focus on making sure that employees do not qualify for costly benefits, Costco goes to great lengths to make sure they get them. For example, they pay for over 90 percent of each employee's health, vision, and dental programs. Most employees, with a few exceptions, qualify for benefits. Unlike their counterparts in the retail industry, the average checker makes over $40,000 per year, plus all those benefits, after 60 months with the company.

Costco is truly one of the smartest companies in America. Their profits and their growth show it. Strategy, organization, and character: that's what high Corporate IQ is all about. Costco's got it all.

Corporate IQ is neither magic nor unfounded fad. Corporate IQ is based on an extensive body of research that links corporate behavior and performance. It's all about maximizing organizational performance . . . and existence. Most importantly, any leader can understand and apply it.

WHAT CREATES SUSTAINABLE SUCCESS?

On any given day, thousands of business people go to a bookstore or to an online site and buy a business book. In almost every case, the motive behind the purchase is to learn about profitability. In some cases, the book may be about total quality or Six Sigma. Others might be about sustainability or some type of scorecard or rating system. At the end of the day, the objective is the same in all cases: creating organizations that enjoy sustainable performance.

One of the challenges that faces business theorists and managers alike is bias or assumptions. As human beings, we intrinsically hate change. In fact, we hate change so much that we will often deny that there's a gorilla in the boardroom in favor of not having to deal with the issue. When it comes to management theory, and corporate strategy as well, we have the same problem. We have grown quite comfortable with the gorilla in the boardroom. So much so, in fact, that we would feel lost without it.

The "gorilla" is management theory as it has existed over the past 100 or so years. When we get down to it, not much has changed. In fact, if you pick up 100 books written about corporate strategy, they will all read and look about the same. The problem? That gorilla—the idea that firms need to focus on, amplify, and improve existing competencies.

This idea has taken many forms over the years, but it is always founded on linear thinking. The concept is that each company has a set of sustainable competencies that can be taken from history into the future. The result of such thinking is comfort. We don't have to think about changing or becoming something different. We just have to become better at what we've always done, regardless of the external environment.

Our basic human desire to avoid change has led us to stay on a path of thinking that allows us to avoid change. That is why the idea of "total quality management" was embraced in the 1980s. Rather than being radical and requiring change, the goal became that of doing what we were already doing, just better than we used to do it. Of course, the excellence movement also appealed to that idea. Out of both came ideas like "best in class" and benchmarking. Again, these ideas created a continuum of process and avoided frame-breaking change.

The problems that companies faced in the late 1980s and early 1990s created a great deal of cognitive dissonance for managers and theorists alike. The idea of sustainable competencies did not seem to fit with reality. In an effort to preserve the status quo of sustainable competencies, a number of people promoted the idea that the problem had to do with change. The result was an avalanche of books, seminars, and speeches about change. All the while, in most cases, these new ideas held on to the concept of sustainable competencies. A few radicals even proposed that occasionally a company might need to adapt its competencies. Business went through a decade or so of change management seminars, and consulting firms established change management practices.

In the 1990s, a few people began to challenge the gorilla in the boardroom idea. It seems that a few radicals thought that the problem involved a thing called "complexity" in the environment. The term *frame-breaking change* was coined. At that time, the management theory camp split and became two camps. One clutching the old theory and its numerous adaptations, and the other suggesting that even the economic theory that founded management thinking needed to be abandoned in favor of one based on complex systems theory.

CHARLES DARWIN EVOLVES AGAIN

This new group of theorists reasoned that the business environment must be a lot like nature. So they borrowed from biology and physics and adopted the ideas of complexity theory and chaos theory. Among the devotees to the concept is Peter Senge, author of *The Fifth Discipline.* Accord to the proponents of this view, organizations must be allowed to self-organize. The result, they hypothesize, is an organization that will upwardly evolve.

Others have rejected the sustainable advantage view and come up with different results. Henry Mintzberg and Ralph Stacey would agree that the business environment is complex and as a result, uncertain. Rather than suggesting a Darwinian approach, both believe that complexity renders the future environment uncertain. As a result of that perspective, they believe in "emergence." As the environment dynamically changes due to complexity issues, the firm must also continually adapt. This incremental adapting is called emergence.

Complexity Yes: Darwinism No

I believe that the evidence is clear when it comes to complexity. The business environment is complex and is continually changing. As a result of that complexity, the organization must also be continually changing. At the same time, there is no evidence that Darwinism or self-organization has any merit. In fact, as you will see later in this book, it will become clear that it has no validity. Similarly, emergence has troubles as well. Success belongs to leaders and organizations that capture the future instead of wait for it to occur. After-the-fact behavior does little more than create a company that is a great follower.

The manager or theorist in search of a way to create maximum sustainable performance may find a dead end. Yet, there are companies, and leaders, who appear to reject the idea of sustainable competencies, Darwinism, and emergence. In most cases, these are successful companies that appear to create long-term sustainable performance. What is it that these companies and their leaders seem to do? Why are they able to adapt to frame-breaking shifts and still keep on going? The answer is found in a term: *mental models.*

HOW YOU THINK IS HOW YOU ACT

Thomas Kuhn, author of *The Structure of Scientific Revolutions*, offered some important observations in his seminal work on mental models. Kuhn concluded that people tend to be locked into their history of training and experience. In fact, he concluded, scientists will often reject evidence they discover that disagrees with their mental model, which is the result of their training.

If the business environment is complex, and it is, then managers must be constantly thinking about differences. The problem is, our minds tend to work on the assumptions of sameness. Kuhn discovered that when a scientist is confronted with hard evidence of difference, they will almost always reject that evidence in favor of a view that supported their view of sameness. The point is that we as human beings tend to reject information about our world if it means we have to work hard to understand it. We embrace sameness.

There is, however, another reality with which we must deal. That is the reality of the external world. Success in business management and strategy has everything to do with a manager's ability to discover the external truth or reality of the business environment. Managers must learn to think in terms of difference instead of sameness. Such thinking is not easy to accomplish, but it is critical to sustainable performance.

THE THREE RULES OF LEADERSHIP AND STRATEGY

Jack Welch established some stringent product portfolio requirements as chairman of GE. One of those was the requirement that GE would divest any business sector in which it was not one of the top three competitors. In late 2002, when the appliances segment became unattractive, the word went out that GE was going to sell its historic cash cow, the appliances division.

Most successful CEOs did not learn how to keep a company on top at a business school. Rather, the cumulative effect of experience, intellect, and intuition allows them to sustain success. In reality, the combination of experience and intellect creates very high levels of intuitive understanding in some individuals. In a lot of cases, these select leaders tend to be natural "systems thinkers." That is, they possess the ability to observe complexity in the business environment and make reliable inferences.

If you read interviews or books by this select group, you will find that they share a distinct pattern of operating and thinking. After studying successful leaders and organizations over a period of years, I have concluded that this pattern of behavior can be summarized into three rules, or the three rules of leadership and strategy. They are as follows:

1. Maximize what's in the box.
2. Think and act out of the box.
3. Stay ahead of the curve.

As you will discover later in this book, the expression of these three rules is somewhat complex. At the same time, the rules are critical for sustainable success. In fact, they might be better identified as the CEO's (or manager's) mission statement. With that in mind, consider the role each of the three rules plays in leadership and corporate strategy.

Maximize What's in the Box

It should surprise no one that most managers and executives have a very simple focus in doing their job. In most cases, they focus on operational issues. They do so for a number of reasons. First, as already pointed out, operational issues are comfortable and familiar. Managers like what's comfortable. Operational issues do not involve change, so that makes them even more appealing. It is probably safe to say that most executives spend over 90 percent of their time on operational issues.

What you will discover about well-run companies is that their leaders do not do that. In fact, you will find that they spend their time balancing their activities equally around the three rule areas. So what does rule #1 really mean?

First of all, in my opinion, great leaders tend to be great philosophers. They are thinkers. In reality, management theory is nothing more than philosophy anyway. It makes sense that the best leaders are the best thinkers.

The first rule is played out in an ability to create an organizational focus on today. This is not a preoccupation with only today, but an ability to focus on maximizing whatever the firm's past innovation efforts have created for you to market. Let's be honest. You can't change today. Today is all you have today, so as a leader you have to find some way to create an organizational focus on maximizing today.

That is most effectively accomplished with excellence. Be careful when you think about this. Certainly excellence has to do with a "commitment to excellence." But it's a lot more.

An organizational focus on maximizing today means that we as an organization must commit to excellence. If your job is sales, you must focus in such a manner that you achieve excellence. If your job is managing others, you must commit to leading others with excellence. Oops! What in the world does that mean? That's a new wrinkle, isn't it?

Commitment to excellence also means commitment to organization. Only people can be committed to an organization. No matter how committed the senior executive team is, without commitment of the rest of the organization, a company will not do well. That means that senior leaders must focus on recognizing the value of every person in the firm, which brings us to a couple of things that need to be understood.

First, the old definition of management, "planning, organizing, leading, and controlling," needs to be replaced. The reality of the complexity of competitive environments requires a new way of thinking about the manager's job. As a result, I have proposed the following definition: "Management is the leading of organizational learning, transformation, and performance." That definition harmonizes with the three rules of leadership and strategy. The result of that mental model is an organization that is capable of maximizing today (rule 1), transforming (rule 2), and maximizing tomorrow (rule 3).

Notice as well that managing is now defined in terms of leadership. Leading infers that there are followers. There is a truism about management and leading. People have little commitment to those who manage them with abrasive power. Organizational commitment to excellence can only occur when people are valued, respected, and recognized by their leaders. That may be why so many of the "best to work for" companies tend to be among the highest performing companies.

In our 1998 book, *The Significance Principle,* Dr. Les Carter and I revealed that an individual's primary motivator is the need to be valued and recognized. We also reveal that most of us build our personal significance at the expense of others. Our conclusion is that senior executives must begin by setting the example of valuing, respecting, and recognizing subordinates. Then they must create a culture of excellence in which every person in the organization is valued, respected, and recognized by their superior or peer. The results of such practices can be phenomenal.

An organizational commitment to excellence in both corporate objectives and in how people are treated creates an organizational focus that produces exceptional results. It gives the organization the ability to maximize today without sacrificing tomorrow.

Think and Act out of the Box

We have all seen it happen. A speaker gets off on a tangent—an idea that they really like—and then forgets their next point. That is what happens if companies are obsessed with the gorilla in the boardroom. Because most of us like feeling comfortable, we have grown comfortable with the gorilla in the boardroom. We really like the idea of a corporate strategy that focuses on what we used to do well, or our "core competencies" and our supposed "competitive advantage."

If the environment is complex and dynamic (notice I added dynamism, or "speed of environmental change" to the formula), and it is, then successful companies are never static. They are constantly changing. As I noted earlier, some hypothesize that leaders cannot anticipate events in complex, dynamic environments, so they propose that we "wait until something happens." Obviously, such an after-the-fact strategy commits the firm to being a consistent follower.

As a researcher for some high-tech international firms, I have found that I often think a lot about the future of computing and telecommunications. A few years ago, I concluded that the future in telecommunications and computers would be in a device I called a FID or "fully integrated device." The FID is a device that combines cell phone, handheld computer, PDA or personal digital assistant, and the World Wide Web. In a number of articles that I wrote, I predicted that soft-switches (a new device manager for all other technologies) would bring paging, office and home voice mail, office and home faxes, cellular communications, and e-mail into one device.

By 2003, it was obvious that I was going to be right. My point is not that I am any different from anyone else. I use what is called "systems thinking" in my research to develop reliable inferences about the future. That means that managers do not have to wait until something happens to formulate a strategy for the future. Just like my understanding of the future of telecommunications, a manager can, and must, be engaged in thinking about the future and how it will be different, not the same.

I was watching the new world champion bull rider being interviewed on a local news network a few years ago. He had been on the rodeo circuit for a number of years and had always been a consistent third or fourth in the rankings. When asked why all of a sudden he became number one, he had a simple but powerful reply: "I realized I had never made the commitment to be number one. I made that commitment, and here I am."

If we as human beings are obsessed with sameness and hate difference, how in the world can we learn to think and act out of the box? The answer is *commitment*. We have to learn to break a habit—and a comfortable one at that. We have to make a personal commitment to excellence in that area, and further, we have to expect those around us in the organization to make a similar commitment.

Unless we lead and encourage others to think and act out of the box, we are failing as managers. In studying some of the best leaders of the past century, I have found that ability is one thing they almost all have in common. They expected their subordinates to act and think out of the box.

Do you realize that the failure to think and act out of the box leads to corporate failure? When we look at some of the great companies that have gone from the top to the bottom over the past 100 years, what one thing did they all have in common? The answer: the environment changed, but they didn't. That was especially true when the total quality movement pounded U.S. companies in the 1980s. It was again true in the 1990s and continues to be true in the 21st century. Companies that fail to adapt in harmony with the external environment cease to exist. Companies that fail to adapt and anticipate environmental shifts are all lacking when it comes to thinking and acting out of the box. It's just that simple.

Dick Bartlett, vice chairman of Mary Kay, Inc., tells the story of how his company dealt with the Internet in the late 1990s. "We knew it had the potential for changing the business landscape," he says. "At the same time, we also recognized that our company's business model had to make sense if we were going to effectively utilize this new marketing medium."

Bartlett calls that time period the "dot-*con*" era. He believes that a lot of fortunes were made at the expense of investors who thought that the Internet alone would make an idea successful. The outcome reveals the wisdom of Bartlett's position and the necessity of having a good business model behind any marketing medium. Few people realize that today, Mary Kay, Inc. is in the top five worldwide among e-business providers.

By thinking and acting out of the box, the Mary Kay organization was able to take a great business model and make it better. They had to rethink their entire recordkeeping, communications, and distribution system. By approaching the opportunity with an out of the box attitude, the firm was able to capitalize on the opportunity. Incidentally, a number of Mary Kay Inc.'s competitors were not so fortunate.

Stay Ahead of the Curve

Ask any executive at an exceptional company what they fear, and you will discover it's the future. Bill Gates, chairman of Microsoft, said he feared the next guy coming down the road with the replacement for his software. Andy Grove, former chairman of Intel, put it simply: "I'm just paranoid."

Great leaders have an ability to continually live in three worlds at the same time: maximizing today, thinking and acting out of the box, and staying ahead of the curve. In the context of my definition of management, great firms and great leaders are always committed to excellence in maximizing today, changing the firm for tomorrow, and anticipating the future. In contrast to their peers at companies going into stagnation, these people are balanced in their focus. They are always obsessed about all three areas, not just about present operations.

Remember my point about the significance principle and how people are valued, respected, and recognized? Great leaders rarely discover the future. Their people do. That is why operationally oriented control freaks do not last very long at most companies. They kill off the creativity and desire to discover the future in their organization. Inside every organization is a group of "sticky note" people. Remember the 3M guy who discovered the sticky note that has now sold in the billions? That product was not invented by a CEO; it was *enabled* by a CEO.

Let's deal with an issue that has been brought up in some circles about CEOs. Some suggest that great organizations are not necessarily led by charismatic, inspirational executives. To put it another way, it doesn't take a charismatic leader to be great. In the strictest sense, that is true. At the same time, those same people tend to diminish the importance of the CEO in achieving success. Nothing could be further from the truth.

Sustainable success is never the result of one component. However, success can be killed by one component, such as the CEO. Among companies that have been recognized for their sustainability, there is a common thread.

The founder of the firm established a strong culture that focused on three things.

1. Maximizing today
2. Thinking and acting out of the box
3. Staying ahead of the curve

In almost every case, those companies have had a succession of CEOs who understood that their job was one of enabling the company to focus on those three areas. In almost every case, the succession of CEOs maintained the founder's commitment to valuing, respecting, and recognizing the people in the firm.

What about the firms that have lasted 100 years or more that don't posses those qualities? They do exist, you know. Those organizations must be recognized and understood to comprehend sustainable success. There are three types of firms that tend to last a long time.

1. Companies with single products that are tied to a 100-year plus demand curve
2. Companies that established and maintained leadership in a product family with a 100-year plus demand curve
3. Companies that were created with a high Corporate IQ and have stayed at that level

In the first instance, some companies are simply lucky enough to be tied to a product that will be in demand for 100 years or more. The firm's founder, due to personal interests and circumstances, decided to enter a business that had a demand cycle in excess of 100 years. End of story. In a number of such cases, the firm does not have a high Corporate IQ. In fact, the market or channel control that the current management of the firm has allows them to break a lot of the Corporate IQ rules and still exist. At the same time, if a frame-breaking shift occurs in the firm's market, one should not expect the firm to do well in the new environment. The firm might not even survive.

It is important to avoid thinking in terms of exception. These are rare companies, not necessarily good ones that enjoy an inherited position. At a number of these companies, people are devalued, and there is little focus on future excellence. They do exist, but their practices do not create sustainable success for companies without their unique position of market control.

The second type of firm is almost identical to the first, except that they are tied to a product family that has a 100-year or more demand cycle. These firms can use channel or distribution control and massive assets to remain competitive in their market segment.

In both cases, it is important to understand that the practices of these companies are not necessary good or profitable for companies in complex, highly competitive environments. Generally, these "old line" companies enjoy a branding advantage as well. It is possible to create brand power, but it costs a lot of money. It takes a lot of money to replace a brand that has been around for 100 years.

That brings us to the third type of firm. High Corporate IQ organizations thrive regardless of product demand cycle. These firms have the ability to become continually something different. Don't get me wrong: if you have the opportunity to attach your firm to a 100-year demand cycle, you would be terminally stupid not to take advantage of an opportunity like that. The reality is, however, those opportunities come along only every 50 years or so. That leaves the average manager with the task of being good. That's the only option for most of us.

The point is, don't fall for the exception. Sure, some companies have been around for a long time, and they are not run according to the three rules of strategy. However, if you look carefully, those companies "happen" to be tied to products or product families that enjoy long demand cycles. It's a little bit like looking at Xerox in the 1960s. They got a 20-year patent that gave them a virtual market monopoly. When the patent expired in 1979, the company entered a less than stellar period that continues through today. It would have been unwise to copy Xerox or some of their supposed "best practices" just because they got lucky on one product.

CORPORATE IQ AND THE THREE RULES

The dean of a prestigious business school once made the following statement: "We get the best and brightest people in the world in our program. My job is to make sure we don't damage them while they're here." That is analogous to Corporate IQ. When we take charge of an organization, it's our job to sustain the organization, not just coercively force out a few quarters or years of profit. Even Attila the Hun can beat a few profitable quarters out of his people. The challenge is sustainability. Further, most of us don't have the luxury of inheriting a company that is tied to products or product families that have 100-year plus demand cycles.

That leaves us with just one thing to do: create or sustain a smart company. Logically, the leader who makes sure that the firm maximizes today, thinks and acts out of the box, and stays ahead of the curve will do just that. Therefore, success is a choice. If you will bear with me, that's exactly what I think you can learn to do. You can learn how to create a high-IQ, smart company that will be even better when you leave. What could be better for you, your employees, your stockholders, or your customers?

4

CONTEXT, CONTEXT, CONTEXT

This chapter may be the most important of this book. The reason is simply that context and profits are inextricably linked. I want to ask you to stop for a moment and think about something. What one assumption seems to underlie most management theories? The answer: "The context will not change."

Take a quick look at one of the most recent bestselling books. What does the author want you to do? The answer: Clone your company to look exactly like a proposed "ideal" company. What is missing from that concept as well as so many others is the reality that a company must fit its context. Here is another reality. Every company's context is different. "Uh oh!" you might say, "Does that mean that if the context for each company is different, that each company must be equally different?"

You already know the answer. That is why ideas like benchmarking so often fail companies. More often than not, the proposed "benchmark" practices of another company are simply not suitable for the benchmarking company. It makes no sense to copy someone else's practice, when you really do not know why you are copying them or, worse yet, whether or not their approach is suitable for your specific corporate challenges.

Earlier, I explained that companies fail because of the phenomena called creative destruction. That is, the creativity of the competition destroys the value of what you currently do as a company. I also suggested that organizations must be adept at dealing with two kinds of forces. First, they must deal with the global environment, or the Ten Forces. Second, they must deal with the segment-specific forces they encounter, generally defined by competitor behavior.

If you think about it, creative destruction is exactly what competitor behavior is all about. One of the greatest delusions that some managers hold is, "I control the market." Not only is that thinking egotistical and a potentially fatal mistake, it is simply not true. Competition is made up of *moments*. Moments are extremely short episodes or events. They are almost like photographs, capturing a scene as part of a changing landscape.

Sustainable success involves an infinite succession of momentary victories.

The whole problem with thinking that involves competitive advantage or supposed core competencies is the "I control the market" fallacy. It may be true for a moment in time that you have some type of an advantage. The problem is, the creative activity of competitors is changing the scenario on a moment-by-moment basis.

SUCCESS VERSUS FAILURE

During one week of reading the business section of my local newspaper, I discovered three compelling examples that illustrate the power that context has over success or failure. In the first example, Fleming Companies was featured. The author of the article examined Fleming, which had almost made the *Fortune* 100 in 2002 only to end up in bankruptcy.

Some might say that their dependence upon K-Mart caused their demise. But insiders suggest that the problem was much bigger than that. Here's what the former CEO said about the demise of the firm:

Fleming is the victim of a flawed business strategy that failed to produce the intended results in a very difficult business environment.[1]

Notice that the problem was the difference between the firm and its context. Simply put, the firm was not suited for its competitive context.

That very same publication featured an article about Kodak just a few days earlier. The article explains that, "Kodak is slashing between 4,500 and 6,000 jobs this year—shrinking its global payroll to about 62,000 from a peak of 136,500 in 1983." That very same article also commented on the root of the problem: "The switch by consumers to digital photography is coming on faster than expected, cutting deeply into the film, paper, and photo finishing businesses that anchor Kodak's profit and image."[2]

A couple of stories need to go along with this. In the early 1990s, Texas Instruments's senior executive team began studying a phenomenon we now call the digital revolution. What the TI executives concluded, almost ten years before the revolution was in full swing, was that this new thing called "digitization" would have a profound effect upon the world as well as on their business. That is why, even though their strategy made little sense to the outsider, the company began selling off profitable businesses to possess the critical mass required for the future business arena of digitization. As is often said, the rest is history. TI is now a global leader in digital signal processor (DSP) technology, a critical component of many telecommunications technologies.

Also in the early 1990s, a man named Michael Sekora was trying to convince Kodak that they had a problem. Some may not be familiar with Sekora. He was the head of Project Socrates for the Reagan administration. It was his job to study global competition and understand what types of strategies American business would face in the future.

After leaving the Reagan administration, Sekora took his skills to the consulting arena. In the early 1990s, he discovered that a competitor of Kodak had created a massive complex of shell companies in America. He began tracing the ownership of each company, and his journey took him to every major technology partner and supplier of Kodak. Sekora discovered that Kodak's Japanese competitor was obtaining all of Kodak's proprietary product information years before the products were to come to market. Here's the unbelievable part of Sekora's story. He could not convince the Kodak executives that the scheme was really happening.

Notice the commonality between Fleming and Kodak. In each case, management had a categorical misunderstanding of the reality that the company faced. That misunderstanding led to totally inappropriate strategy. Context is critical—this is an unavoidable reality for business. Smart companies are impacted by extreme shifts in the competitive context just like other companies. One company that was severely hit by the technology meltdown of 2001 and 2002 was Agilent Technologies, one of the top ten smartest companies in America.

AGILENT TECHNOLOGIES: ONE OF THE TEN SMARTEST COMPANIES IN AMERICA

Agilent, like other technology companies, suffered in the aftermath of the combined impact of the post–9/11 economy and the technology meltdown of the same period. It would be an understatement to suggest that Agilent's industry segment went through a frame-breaking shift in its environment. The difference between smart companies and their counterparts is how they come out of such frame-breaking shifts.

In late 2003, while discussing the top ten smartest companies list, my editor questioned just how wise it was to put a company that was (at that time) losing a lot of money on such a list. I confidently explained to him that Corporate IQ was a great predictor of a company's future performance. In the first quarter of 2004, Agilent proved me right, as they turned the corner and again entered a time of sustained profitability.

Agilent was a spin-off from Hewlett-Packard in 1999. Its leadership spent a great deal of time making sure that the founding principles of the company were kept intact. The company's management makes sure that every member of the Agilent team understands just how critical his or her role is for the overall success of the firm. The company's CEO has spent the months since the spin-off visiting with Agilent's people around the world. To date, he's managed to meet with over 80 percent of the company's almost 30,000 people.

Agilent focuses on highly aggressive innovation activities as well as equally aggressive marketing strategies. The organization features an employee-focused culture that ensures a customercentric focus. Like all smart companies, it is founded upon an exceptional commitment to the highest standards of corporate character.

Context is the issue. Competitive life is not a succession of repetitive events. It is a succession of different events. The companies that succeed over long periods are those that continually anticipate the uncertainty of change by constantly changing how and where they compete.

Hopefully, the reality of context is influencing your thinking. The reason that most management theories fall flat is that they are based on what I call "simple stability." In other words, the theorist assumes that the compet-

> There is no such thing as competitive advantage. Winning is a succession of winning and losing moments, in which the top company simply had more winning moments than their competitors.

itive world will be simple, not complex, and constant instead of varying in speed (of change). Let me ask you to stop and think about this for just a moment. I will assume that you support the ideas of core competencies, competitive advantage, and mission (in the box) thinking. Let me ask you a question: can you name any competitors who compete using a simple, stable mental model in developing their strategy? Of course, the question reveals the problem. It is simply not reality. Competitors stay awake at night trying to create better products, decrease cycle times, and beat you in the marketing arena. That is simply fact—and it's what creative destruction is all about. Either you choose to win, or your competitor will win.

> "I guess the environment changed and we didn't."

The former CEO of an internationally recognized company made this statement. The company no longer exists. The reason: They failed to account for global changes as well as the changes in the ways that their competitors were going to market. Companies fail because they fail to match changes in competitor behavior.

CONTEXT: A NEW WAY OF THINKING

Thomas Kuhn crystallized much of the reality of paradigms. In many ways, his 1970 work, *The Structure of Scientific Revolutions,* runs parallel to Schumpeter's work on creative destruction. On one hand, Schumpeter suggests that competitive reality involves a succession of destructive events driven by the creativity of competitors. On the other hand, Kuhn reveals that the human mind tends to reject such change, even though it is reality. It should surprise no one that top-performing organizations tend to be led by managers who correctly perceive the complexity and speed of their competitive environments.

In Chapter 1, I discussed the work of John W. Sutherland. He proposed four types of environments.

1. Deterministic (highly predictable)
2. Moderately variable (mostly predictable)
3. Severely variable (generally unpredictable)
4. Indeterminate (totally unpredictable)[3]

Let's use Sutherland's four types of environments to take a brief look forward at Corporate IQ. They will help us understand how context relates to the company and how it can have a critical impact on a nonadaptive organization.

It is somewhat obvious, even to the casual observer, that a firm with a linear mentality (focusing upon historic competencies) will have numerous problems in what Sutherland calls an indeterminate environment. In that worst-case context, the firm's competitors will be continually altering the rules of the game. While the competitors are creating numerous new products every year and introducing them with a take no prisoners marketing strategy, our nonadaptive company will compete much as though they are going for a walk in the park. They will be mugged numerous times before they manage to get through the park. The company simply lacks the ability to compete like its competitors. That is the problem.

WHAT IS AMBIGUITY?

It's difficult to define. I'm not being funny, but that's what the word generally means. *Ambiguity,* historically conveying the fact that a word may have multiple meanings, has become increasingly used in business. Another word that defines ambiguity is *cloudiness.* A pilot friend once described instrument flying as an experience similar to "flying in a bowl of milk." In other words, you are flying without a lot of visual clues to attitude, altitude, or speed.

When you get down to it, ambiguity is the reason behind so many books on management and strategy. It's also why there are so many different ideas about how to manage an organization. The environment has become increasingly ambiguous, spawning a lot of ideas about how to deal with it. Here are just a few.

- Scenarios
- Contingency planning
- Game theory
- War gaming
- Emergence
- Complex adaptive systems
- Systems thinking
- Hybrids (combinations of two or more of the above)

A lot of people have studied the relationships between how people think and how effectively they manage and lead an organization. The reality is, the better or more accurately you perceive competitive reality, the better you manage. The end result of matching the right mental model with reality is high corporate performance.

DISCOVERING REALITY IN AMBIGUITY

A number of theorists suggest that the level of ambiguity in today's complex environments, or systems, is just too much for the human mind to comprehend. Ralph Stacey and Henry Mintzberg are two such theorists. They base their ideas on a concept called "bounded rationality." The result of such thinking is an idea that I call "emergence." That is, rather than thinking about the future, wait until events occur and then respond. In other words, it is impossible to plan for complexity, so just wait until something happens.

Lofti Zadeh developed the term *fuzzy logic*. Rather than interpreting an idea in terms of absolute rights or wrongs, he suggested that propositions may have degrees of truth or falsity.[4] There are absolutes, but at the same time I believe Zadeh may be on the right track in a number of ways, especially as it relates to the ideas of Mintzberg and Stacey.

It is possible to make inferences about complex situations. We do that all the time. Can we predict exact events? No, but we can predict the nature of events. In a number of speeches prior to 9/11, I suggested that it was not a question of whether we would experience a terrorist attack in the United States, it was only a question of when. I made those predictions in 2000.

My graduate students have been extremely accurate in predicting the future environment for over 100 *Fortune* 500 companies. Generally, they have not predicted specific events, but at the same time they have quite accurately predicted the nature of the future competitive environment for those companies.

COMPETITOR INDEX

In studying under H. Igor Ansoff, one of the first things I had to learn about was what he called "environmental turbulence." While Ansoff has been recognized as the "father of strategic management," I'd footnote that title to recognize his work in the area of complexity as well as change in the competitive environment. That is what his work on environmental turbulence was all about.[5]

The Ansoff scale of environmental turbulence is comprised of two subsets: marketing turbulence and innovation turbulence. The absolute brilliance of Ansoff's work is apparent for a couple of reasons. First, he understood clearly that all of a firm's success strategy had to be driven by competitor's behavior. Second, almost as if he had read Schumpeter's mind when it came to creative destruction, Ansoff accounted for it by measuring the innovation behavior or turbulence in a competitive segment.

John Sutherland's "four states of the environment" is very insightful. At the same time, it is probably fair to say that Sutherland is describing the result of competitor activity as opposed to the basic drivers of environmental conditions. That's where Ansoff's work is so beneficial. Over the past few years, I've adapted Ansoff's approach to reflect a few changes that I discovered in my research. At any rate, here is the end result of that work.[6] The first of two components of environmental turbulence is marketing turbulence.

When we look at any competitive segment, we are most interested in competitor behavior. It's also important to remember that, when we measure this in the external environment, we will never have any area that measures as a round number. It's usually something like 3.7 or 4.2. That is why an analysis of this type involves a lot of study and intuitive reflection. It's not a simple process.

In trying to determine marketing turbulence, we might find that sales aggressiveness (of competitors) is 4.1, marketing aggressiveness (sales and PR) is 3.6, marketing strategy is 4.4, and the demand/capacity ratio is 4.5.

FIGURE 4.1   *Marketing Turbulence*

MARKETING TURBULENCE

Competitor Index	1	2	3	4	5
Sales aggressiveness	Low		Competitive		Highly aggressive
Marketing aggressiveness	Low		Competitive		Very high
Marketing strategy	Serve customers		Grow market		Expand share
Industry capacity versus demand	Excess demand		Equilibrium		Excess capacity

To determine marketing turbulence, we would then average the values to come up with one number.

A Technical Word of Caution

To avoid confusing the reader, I've purposely avoided discussing a number of issues about turbulence. First, turbulence is always measured in the future if we are developing future strategy. Without going into the multiple measurement approaches used for estimating future turbulence, I will simply say it is fairly complex, extremely comprehensive, and, as a result, quite accurate. On a number of occasions, clients have retained me for the sole purpose of predicting future turbulence for a segment, so that they would better understand what to expect from their competitors. That said, I will continue to speak of turbulence in the present instead of the future, just so you won't be confused.

The second determinate of environmental turbulence is innovation turbulence. I've mentioned "creative destruction" a number of times in the first few chapters of this book. It should come as no surprise that Ansoff brilliantly included competitor innovation in his approach. The following table shows my adapted version of innovation turbulence.

Innovation turbulence reveals the level and aggressiveness of competitor innovation. As the level of turbulence increases, the frequency of events of creative destruction increases. Again, we will generally discover that each measurement is different.

Once we have both environmental turbulence and innovation turbulence, we average them to obtain what I call the competitor index. In other words, we now have a number that conveys a wealth of information. I would

FIGURE 4.2   *Innovation Turbulence*

INNOVATION TURBULENCE[7]					
Competitor Index	**1**	**2**	**3**	**4**	**5**
Innovation aggressiveness	Low		Competitive		Highly innovative
Technological change	Slow		Fast		Extremely fast
Innovation strategy	Product duplication		Product improvement		Product innovation
Customer strategy	Meet needs		Stay close to the customer		Anticipate unrealized needs
Product life cycles	Long		Moderate		Very short

like to discuss the important contribution that an accurately measured competitor index can play in the strategy of a company.

SYSTEMS THINKING

Although he never mentioned it when developing his system, Ansoff was really creating a highly sophisticated systems thinking model. The idea behind systems thinking, as I mentioned earlier, is that one can make reliable inferences about complex environments. What the Ansoff model accomplished was a highly accurate systems thinking approach in which each critical slice of the future environment is measured.

Most management theorists know that there is a problem called paradigm blindness. It is a recognized fact that most people will reject changes in the competitive environment, no matter how well supported by evidence, in favor of how things "used to work." Most people prefer sameness in lieu of difference when it comes to thinking about the competitive environment. One company that is exceptionally good at understanding its context is Mary Kay, Inc. Mary Kay, Inc. is one of the top ten smartest companies in America.

MARY KAY INC.: ONE OF THE TEN SMARTEST COMPANIES IN AMERICA

I must confess, when I was first granted access to this company in 2002, I really did not expect to find one that was so creative and aggressive and, at the same time, had such exceptional levels of corporate character. One of the first things I found was that the company is constantly challenging the limits of innovation.

Mary Kay's people spend a great deal of time in trying to anticipate changing customer needs. They do that by not only doing a lot of research but also by spending a great deal of time listening to the independent sales force and their customers. The result is an organization known for its ability to anticipate trends.

Like the other smart companies, Mary Kay Inc. insists that leadership practices should create a place where people want to work. At the heart of the philosophy of the company's founder, Mary Kay Ash, was the Golden Rule. By maintaining Mary Kay's philosophy, the company has continued to thrive.

A lot of people have no idea of just how leading edge this company is. Over the years, the company has pioneered new approaches to manufacturing and inventory management. In the early 2000s, Mary Kay Inc. became one of the top e-businesses in the world. Since that time, the organization has continued to devote resources to achieve technological leadership in the direct selling industry.

In 2001, the company lost its founder, Mary Kay Ash. Some suggested that her death would set the company back. As with other smart leaders, Mary Kay had planned to make sure that the character and the traditions of her company would continue long after her passing. By 2004, the company was nearing $2 billion in retail sales, had passed the 1 million mark in number of independent beauty consultants, was experiencing rapid revenue growth in the international market, and was breaking every sales record the company had ever set. Truly, Mary Kay Inc. deserves the title of "one of the ten smartest companies in America."

Clearly events of creative destruction radically change the rules of the game. The products the firm used to make, the business the firm was in, and sometimes even the entire family of products that are the foundation of the firm's business no longer are the object of consumer demand. In other words, you may make the best buggy whip in the business, but there are simply no buyers for the fruit of your "core competencies."

The result of Ansoff's work is a highly accurate and practical approach to applying systems thinking to corporate strategy. Because the approach measures numerous slices of the competitive environment, the synthesized result of the approach is a highly accurate tool for managers.

OOPS . . . WHY DID WE FIRE HIM?

One of the first thing a consultant has to recognize is that they will often be fired for doing some of their best work. If a consultant walks in the door of a new client and discovers a major problem, chances are it's not news to the company. In most cases, a number of people have been trying to tell the leadership about the problem for some time. The problem most consultants have to face is that they will usually get fired for pointing out the problem.

One of the things I have discovered in my work with companies in trouble is that they almost always have a leadership problem. The symptoms are often most evident in areas like sales, innovation, and the like, but the bottom line is usually the problem in leadership. If you think about it, a problem in sales or innovation can almost always be traced to the leadership of the firm.

> We have discovered the problem . . . and it is you!

At one client, I found out just how difficult it is to get an organization to face reality. The firm was facing one of those creative destruction events. Its entire industry was on the verge of a major overhaul. My study of the future environment had made that problem quite clear, right down to the technology that would replace my client's technology.

The real problem I faced, however, was not a dramatic shift in the competitive environment. The real problem was an entire organization, from top to bottom, that was committed to maintaining the status quo. They were willing to lie and do just about anything else to make sure that nothing changed.

After I was shown the door, I did try to get this critical information back into the company through some personal contacts. The level of arrogance I encountered was unbelievable. No one in the organization was willing to try to get the critical information to the right people. They all feared for their jobs. Ironically, almost all of those jobs went away as a result of the failure to address this specific issue.

This is one case in which I really would have preferred to be wrong. The sad truth is, however, that the company was devastated less than four years later, when the technological revolution that I'd predicted hit.

Although not always successful in overcoming resistance to change, the analysis that leads to a competitor index can often be eye opening for a leadership team. In one futuristic study I did in 1996, I predicted major changes in an area called SOHO (small office home office). Not only did the research reveal that the trend toward SOHOs was substantial, but further that the demand for broadband technologies at home was going to explode. In this case, the client company listened and used the competitor index as a basis for their future technology focus.

CONTEXT, CONTEXT, CONTEXT

The October 6, 2003, *Newsweek* carried a short but important article. Titled "A New 'Wind Tunnel' for Companies," its thrust was how major global companies are trying to find ways to predict the future environment. The major point was simply that if companies could predict the future (context), they could be more profitable.

I have good news for you. It is possible to predict the future context, and yes, the research makes it clear that those who most accurately understand future context lead more profitable companies. Einstein once suggested that if you have one week to solve a problem, spend the first six days understanding it.

Strategy, contrary to the thinking in some circles, must follow context. That is the missing link in management thinking today. Context also determines what type of organization we need to deploy to maximize profit. When you get right down to it, this is the only logical conclusion. If context defines competitor behavior, your firm will succeed or fail based on whether or not you profile your firm for that competitive index. Most importantly, competitor index gives the manager a valid systems thinking approach from which to consider the firm's strategic future.

Often, at the end of an hour's television program, the announcer will come on and tell you why you should stay tuned. They will explain that the program coming up next is really interesting. I would like to suggest that about the next few chapters. You will find that it is possible to custom-design your company to fit the competitive context. It's all about performance. It can change the way you look at your job as a leader and, more importantly, can change the future of your firm.

5

CUSTOM-BUILT COMPANIES

One of the most eye-opening and powerful moments in most managers' lives is when they discover the reality of business competition. It is eye opening, because it is the antithesis of what they have been taught about corporate profitability. It is powerful, because from that point forward, they will have a much better grasp of how to maximize profit.

Think back for a moment about what I have been discussing in this book. Business environments undergo constant changes in speed and complexity. That's important to remember. In the previous chapter, I developed the idea of the competitive environment extensively, but for communication purposes, I'd like to simplify it. Let's assume for a moment that the business environment can only exist in three states.

1. Slow, simple
2. Fast, moderately complex
3. Overwhelming speed and complexity

In your opinion, would the firm designed to maximize profit in the slow-simple environment maximize profit in the fast-complex environment? Would the firm designed to excel in the overwhelming environment do well in the slow-simple environment?

I want you to think about this seriously. It's really important. Neither firm would do well in the other environment. The firm designed for the slow-simple environment would lack the speed, aggressiveness, and adaptive abilities to compete in the overwhelming, rapidly changing environment. At the same time, the firm designed for the overwhelming environment would be much too aggressive for the slow-simple environment. It would significantly overspend in strategic areas such as marketing and product development (R&D).

What you discovered in the previous chapter is that a company may compete in almost infinite types of environments. That means that the business leader's role in managing a company is to understand two things.

1. What types of environment will the firm face?
2. What must the company look like to maximize profit?

I want to give you a little sneak preview of exactly what Corporate IQ can do for you. First, it gives you a powerful, intuitive tool for understanding the competitive environment. Second, it provides you a detailed plan from which you can custom design your company for that environment. If you were not yet convinced, I would like to offer you just one statistic from the research that Igor Ansoff and his associates conducted over the past 30 years.[1]

> Companies that match their competitive context, versus those that do not, have a return on investment that is 100 to 300 percent higher.

Corporate IQ is built upon the research begun by Ansoff and his associates. What Ansoff hypothesized (and was later confirmed by research) was that companies may be broken down into two broad areas, strategy (two attributes) and organization (six attributes), and if those areas were well matched with the competitive environment, the firm would be more profitable. In my studies over the past ten years, I concluded that three broad areas needed to be used: strategy, organization, and character. I also increased the number of attributes measured from 8 to 17.

Here is where it gets really interesting. Earlier, I noted Jim Collins and Jerry Porras's comments in *Built to Last*. As they said, in a lot of the "excellence" books, the authors made observations at excellent companies and computed mathematical averages around different attributes that they hoped would reveal the secret to performance or sustainability. The idea was to measure attributes of the excellent companies to discover the reasons for their success. This was often done by using massive studies that resulted in a comparison of statistical averages. Collins and Porras had pointed out that all of the successful companies have a building. By using simple statistical averages, the researchers were suggesting that they had discovered the keys to performance. Collins and Porras were pointing out that the use of such averages would also lead one to conclude that all excellent companies have a building, for example. Obviously, that is simply not a good research strategy for understanding corporate performance.

In the research conducted by Ansoff and his associates, as well as my Corporate IQ research, a significant emphasis was placed on statistical relationships. For those who do not spend a great deal of time with statistics, let me explain this a little further.

If you were conducting research on the causes of cancer and found that all of those who got cancer had a specific gene, and all of those who did not lacked that gene, you might have discovered important information. The problem in research is to try to distill the cause-and-effect relationship of phenomena. In the case of corporate excellence studies, the average might have some meaning, but certainly is not a clear indicator of a cause-and-effect relationship.

The Stage I research project for my Corporate IQ measurement involved 15 companies. My hypothesis was simply that companies with a higher Corporate IQ would have a higher decile ranking (top 10 percent, second 10 percent, etc.) than those with a low Corporate IQ. Corporate IQ is a comprehensive assessment that measures 17 broad areas of the firm. The following are the results of that first study. Because I had to get internal access to the companies, I agreed to keep the participants' names anonymous. Many are publicly traded, so that stipulation made a lot of sense.

	CIQ	Rank
Financial Org	157	2
Entertainment Co.	140	3
Energy Co.	146	1
Telecommunications	40	10
Transportation	155	1
Consumer Goods	167	1
Training Org.	58	10
Investments	152	1
Technology	120	2
Financial Org	154	1
Int'l Financial Org.	119	2
Mortgage Co.	145	2
Chemicals	134	2
Telecommunications	160	2
Tech Mfg.	95	6

The statistical analysis of these companies' rankings confirms what is also clear to the casual observer. In regard to all of the companies that I have had the opportunity to measure, I discovered that the higher the Corporate IQ, the higher the decile ranking of the competitor.

Cause-and-effect relationships are nearly impossible to determine. Researchers try to develop statistical relationships. For example, let's assume that you could compare the leadership style of managers at 20 high ROI (return on investment) companies and 20 low ROI companies. It would be possible to develop a statistical relationship that provides relationships between ROI and leadership style. That is quite different from a simple average. Establishing a statistical relationship is important to you as a manager as well. If the research is done well, it can be a powerful tool for understanding organizational performance. Averages, as Collins and Porras point out, may shed some light on a subject but fall short of any type of definitive evidence of profitability.

THE BEDROCK PRINCIPLE OF PROFIT AND PERFORMANCE

If you were to ask yourself (or anyone for that matter) about the question that is behind almost every management book written, what would that question be? Simply put, it would have to be the following: how can a company maximize profit? Here are some of the proposed answers that have come forward over the past 20 years.

- Focus on the firm's historic competencies.
- Be a total quality management organization.
- Have an adaptive culture.
- Lead like Attila the Hun.
- Open your books to the employees.
- Maximize the company's resources.
- Focus on the value chains in your industry.
- Adopt the best practices of other companies.
- Cut cycle times.
- Be excellent, whatever that is.
- Form teams.
- Downsize your way to success.

I won't bore you with the technical details, but basically there is no hard evidence that any of the above is a "single solution" that will create success. That leaves us with an unanswered question: how can a company maximize its profit?

THE MISSING LINK

In 1977, Alfred Chandler, in his landmark work *The Visible Hand,* proposed that business success is rooted in a business structure.[2] He suggested that the foundation to a firm's competitiveness related more to a firm's structure than to anything else and that strategy must follow structure.

In Chandler's work, as well as with almost all other management theorists' thinking of the last 100 years, there is a missing link. The missing link is not the dominance that an appropriate organizational structure can impose on an industry or how some set of best practices can do the same. To propose that is to miss the very essence of business competition. The essence, the missing link, is simply that all business thinking must begin with environment. Environment must drive strategy. In addition, environment must drive organization, including structure.

Please allow me to reach into my background in logic and philosophy. Environment is simply what *is*. One can describe the condition of the surroundings or environment of the firm. In fact, they are generally described in terms of competition. A firm succeeds or fails based, not on its structure, but on whether or not the entire firm is well suited to "what is." That is, to its environment.

If that is true, and it is, quality and/or "Six Sigma" approaches will generally change or improve what the firm used to do, without any consideration of possible frame-breaking changes that might slam into the organization. Here's a challenge: name a firm that has failed and ask why. The answer: The firm failed because competitors changed the way they were doing business and the firm did not.

Why has K-Mart continued to struggle? Because K-Mart has never been able to raise its organization to the competitive capability of its competitors. Yes, structure is involved, but so is marketing, innovation, strategy, culture, management, technology, etc. Across the board, K-Mart has been unable to correct those problems.

I have said this numerous times already, but I feel compelled to say it once more. The business environment is complex, as is the organization. As much as we would like to think that a simple solution will fix a complex entity, it simply will not. Every part of that complex machine we call a company has got to be in sync with the firm's context or competitive environment. If it is not, the firm will experience deteriorating performance and possibly cease to exist. It all gets down to the environment.

In the previous chapter, I discussed the idea of the environment and what I call the competitor index. Again, the idea is to use a five-point scale to indicate the level of complexity and the rate of change in the environment. Please remember that the competitor index is a descriptive metaphor of what the competitors in any given segment will be doing. Logically, the competitor index, if accurately measured, tells the manager exactly what the company must do to compete and maximize profit. An overwhelming amount of research demonstrates the truth of that idea.

Once we understand the competitor index of our company's segment, we also begin to understand something else. All of the other answers to the question about maximizing profit cannot be right. It becomes astoundingly clear. To maximize profit, our company must match that competitive index, or it will fail. To put it another way, if the company's behavior is less aggressive and less adaptive than its competitors', it will not succeed. As I said earlier, in contrast to Alfred Chandler's proposal that "strategy must follow structure," solving problems is much more involved. I want you to consider that the following three areas—corporate strategy, organization, and character—are each made up of numerous components. With that in mind, here are the three rules of competitive success.

The **R**u l e s o f **C**o m p e t i t i v e **S**u c c e s s

1. Strategies must match competitor index.
2. Organization must match competitor index.
3. Organizational character must be maximized.

I would like to visit each of these areas individually. To maximize profit, a manager must thoroughly understand them.

STRATEGIES MUST MATCH THE COMPETITOR INDEX

Let's assume for the moment that the competitor index is 4.8. As you may remember, that is a competitive environment of extremely rapid change with high levels of uncertainty, overwhelming competition, and very short product life cycles. Let's take a look at the strategies your organization will need to be successful.

- Extremely aggressive sales, public relations, and advertising.
- Extremely high levels of innovation (new products, etc.).
- A product portfolio with a preponderance of products focused on phases I and II of the product life cycle.
- A significant focus on the inclusion and application of technology in all products and services.

Let's assume for a moment that you are tempted to focus more on the firm's core competencies. After all, that's a lot easier way to run a company, isn't it? Easier, yes, but is it smarter? No.

The Components of Strategy

- Marketing aggressiveness
- Innovation aggressiveness
- Product portfolio balance
- Product technology applications

Regardless of your firm's core competencies, if you fail to match the competitor's behaviors, you will not succeed in the emerging environment. That is why companies fail. Their competitors out-innovate and out-market them, as the firm simply fails to respond because its focus is on the past, not the present or the future. It is a matter of straightforward fact: strategies must match the competitor index.

ORGANIZATIONS MUST MATCH THE COMPETITOR INDEX

The strategies allow the firm to create competitive discontinuities in the lives of competitors. Strategy is the firm's attempt to destroy creatively the value of the competitors' product portfolio and to replace it with the firm's own solution. That is the story of competition. The provider of one set of products and services is continually trying to come up with new and different ways to meet customer needs. At the same time, so are all of the competitors in that segment. The result is a continual re-creation of the segment through creative destruction events that come from competitor innovation.

The firm must not only continually thrust its creative efforts into the marketplace, it must be able to adapt simultaneously to the creative thrusts of competitors. So what we end up with is a company that is continually innovating and changing the rules of the game and, at the same time, adapting to changes resulting from competitors' thrusts. It's a little bit like walking and chewing gum at the same time. It's not an either-or situation—it's both. The successful firm must have the proactive capabilities to attack competitors' product offerings, while at the same time being highly adaptive in responding to competitors' thrusts.

Now let's look at how this plays out in the real world. What do Motorola, Xerox, and Kodak all have in common? They all have cultures that focus on maintaining the status quo. The problem is, all three are in competitive segments in which the competitive index is around level 4 and above. Their competitors are continually changing the competitive landscape, while Motorola, Kodak, and Xerox have a culture that enforces "no change."

The Components of Organization

- CEO attributes
- Management
- Culture
- Structure
- Decision systems (early warning systems; speed)
- Strategy
- Creative capacity
- Product technology applications

If a firm is not only to possess sustainability but also maximize profit, all of the components of the organization must align with the competitor index.

The Components of Organizational Character

- Ethics
- Excellence rating
- Value of people
- Quality and process
- Values

DO WE NEED CUSTOM-BUILT COMPANIES?

Earlier, I mentioned John W. Sutherland's proposal that there were four distinct conditions of the competitive environment. I would like to use his ideas as a basis for understanding the importance of Corporate IQ and designing a company around an environment. Here are the four environmental conditions that Sutherland developed.

1. Deterministic (highly predictable)
2. Moderately variable (mostly predictable)
3. Severely variable (generally unpredictable)
4. Indeterminate (totally unpredictable)[3]

Now let's just think about what type of organization will be needed for a firm to succeed in each type of environment. I will simply use the three broad areas of the firm as my basis for comparison: strategy, organization, and character.

1. Deterministic (Highly Predictable)

- *Strategies.* Because the firm's context is totally predictable, my strategies can be simple with no risk required. I can also keep my innovation at fairly low levels and create new products on an as needed basis. Certainly I do not need to be aggressive in any area of my strategies, because I can accurately predict my competitors' every move.
- *Organization.* The firm's structure can be a strict and steep bureaucracy. Management can be highly controlling, and the firm's culture can focus on maintaining the status quo. The firm has little need for adaptive capabilities, because the emerging environment is so predictable. Rewards can be objectives-based (MBOs), because such a high level of predictability makes it possible to set quantitative goals and expect success if the employee carries them out.
- *Character.* Character involves issues that control how the firm does business. Questionable ethics may reap a few quarters or even years of increased profits, but at the same time, such behavior can ultimately destroy the firm. Integrity is the foundation of trust, and regardless of the external environment, solid principles always underlie workforce stability and interpersonal transactions.

  Another aspect of character is "value of subordinates." Not only is it possible to measure the level of value of subordinates, but the data suggests a direct link between such behavior and organizational performance. Regardless of the level of external competitiveness, companies that communicate that they value their employees—and walk the talk—will be more profitable. Character, and its five components, are the only aspect of the firm that is not context dependent.

2. Moderately Variable

In a moderately variable context, the firm's *strategies* must be stepped up a bit. Approaches like benchmarking and best practices can work quite well at this level. In a moderately variable environment, creative destruction events are few and far between. Notice also that the firm's product portfolio should be skewed toward product life cycle stages III and IV (maturity and decline). At this level of competitive context, leading is not much needed because in a context of low rates of change and complexity, following is much more profitable.

The *organization* itself can be designed for stability. A divisional structure will work nicely. The culture, including rewards systems, can focus on stability issues. Corporate strategy (approaches) can also utilize linear types of thinking, because environmental change is mostly predictable. Corporate intelligence of the futuristic type is not much needed, but the firm may need to get involved in some simplistic business intelligence activities.

It's important to remember that a moderately variable environment will provide few surprises. Competitors are mostly predictable, and to do otherwise (overinnovate and overmarket) would do little more than lower profits and shorten product life cycles.

Character, as previously mentioned, provides stability for the firm and should not change as the firm's context changes. An absence of the highest levels of character can destroy a firm, regardless of the level of competition.

3. Severely Variable

Let's stop and think for a minute. If an environment is severely variable, obviously competitive forces are driving that particular context. The creative activities of competitors are producing somewhat frequent events of creative destruction.

As we think further about this particular context, sustainability has everything to do with a firm's ability to be something different continually, rather than to focus upon sameness or historic competencies. That should help explain why some of the thinking in the field of strategy, such as the equilibrium-based view (historic competencies) or the resource view (leverage existing resources, still an historic mental model), tend to fail organizations. To put it another way, the long-term survival of the firm is totally dependent upon its ability to deliver events of creative destruction, in the form of new products or new business arenas, to its competitors.

> As the competitive context becomes severely variable,
> the firm must have strategies that fit the environment.

At the same time, the competitive thrusts characteristic of such an environment inevitably drive numerous environmental surprises for the firm. The adaptive capabilities of the organization minimize the financial impact of such discontinuities. A nonadaptive culture, an inflexible structure, and a stability-focused senior executive are just some of the aspects that can kill the firm in that context.

Severely variable environments require high levels of adaptive thinking. A "maintain the status quo" culture must be replaced by a "challenge everything" culture. Rewards must focus on the level of creativity instead of the usual MBOs that worked in a more predictable environment. Corporate strategy must be nonlinear, and early warning systems (corporate intelligence) are a must. The objective is not only discontinuous thinking and behavior but speed of response as well.

4. Indeterminate

The best way to describe an indeterminate context is "your worst nightmare." At that level, competitor creativity and, thus, events of creative destruction are extremely high. Additionally, the speed of change can be overwhelming. It's not like you are fighting just one enemy who just keeps throwing different weapons at you; they are adding more speed to their thrusts as well.

Strategy at this level of competition must allow for mistakes. In fact, unless a firm is making some mistakes, it is probably not being creative or aggressive enough. Earlier in the book, I talked about how managers should think about their firm. I talked about managers viewing themselves as managers of a stock portfolio instead of managing in a specific business sector.

This explains why concepts such as the "resource view" of the firm can be so problematic in indeterminate environments. You will also remember that the second rule of strategy and leadership is to "think and act out of the box." In an indeterminate environment, that type of thinking can create a firm that achieves long-term performance.

The only resource a firm has, in reality, are its assets. The issue is not what factories you have and how you can leverage them; it is how much are those assets worth? Let's be realistic about something. It is always costly to move from one area of business to an entirely different area. But remember: it can often be more costly to fail to move to an entirely new area of business.

> In extreme circumstances, success often depends upon a firm's ability to move to radically different and more profitable areas.

From a dynamics standpoint, the *organization* must be poised to adapt aggressively. At this level of competition, only companies that eat change for breakfast will ultimately survive. Field managers often have little time to call the home office and ask permission to implement a new strategy. As the old saying goes, "It's easier to ask for forgiveness than permission."

Organizational character plays a critical role in this context. The people in an organization of necessity must be continually trying new ideas that will pique the customer's interest. People must unquestionably trust their superiors when it comes to supporting them when they make mistakes. Mistakes are a given at this level of uncertainty.

Let me add a comment here about risk. There is smart risk and there is stupid risk. Learning organizations are also teaching organizations, and the people who have to do the teaching are the frontline managers. I have personally demonstrated that it is possible to teach subordinates to take risk as well as the difference between smart and stupid risk. Regardless, there has to be a safety net of trust, encouragement, and support to catch those contributors who make mistakes. An exceptional company that seems to effectively combine aggressiveness and responsiveness is Kingston Technology, one of the top ten smartest companies in America.

KINGSTON TECHNOLOGY: ONE OF THE TEN SMARTEST COMPANIES IN AMERICA

Can you imagine working at a company where the CEO periodically challenged you to be creative and take a risk? What if that same CEO took the blame if the idea did not turn out too well? Would you believe it if someone told you there was a company that expected its people to take action before they asked for permission? On top of all that, could you ever believe that such a company could be one of the top performers in its industry?

You might not believe any of these things could be true unless, that is, you have spent time at Kingston Technology in Irvine, California. "The first thing I had to do when I came to work at Kingston," said one manager, "was to forget everything I'd learned in my MBA." The people at Kingston break all the rules simply because that is the rule.

Kingston is an international leader in the area of computer memory. The company combines leading edge customer service, speed-of-light processes, and ahead-of-the-curve strategies to create one of the most loyal customer bases on the globe. While competitors strive for a 30-day ship time, Kingston often provides same-day service for customers located in their immediate area.

At Kingston, you will find the employee and customer focus that is so characteristic of high-performing, smart companies. In a highly diverse workplace, Kingston's leadership is able to take advantage of the broad cultural differences of its people to consider all possible approaches for better serving customers. Among leading edge companies, Kingston is just about as leading edge as it gets.

CUSTOM-BUILT COMPANIES

I don't like authors who set out to gain at the expense of others. I don't think anyone gains if one sets out to do that. At the same time, there is a tension that exists between books on the same topic. As I said earlier, the bottom line is how to maximize profit.

I know that some of the things that I am saying will appear to be (and are) critical of others' ideas. At the same time, it should be clear that what I am suggesting is radically different from their ideas. As hard as I might try to harmonize with others' ideas, I must face the fact that my proposal for how to maximize profit is different. In fact, it is radically different. I hope you will keep in mind the fact that I believe those with whom I am differing are generally very bright people. I truly respect them for their intellect.

The debate that surrounds the approaches to corporate management and strategy involves numerous different ideas that are clearly in conflict with each other. From that standpoint, I am no different than the rest. That's why they write books. That's also why I must engage in the debate about profit maximization. In some ways, the course of nations and the lives of people depend on how companies are managed. If you don't think that is true, just investigate the lives of those who lose their jobs when a company fails.

With that said, the rest of this book is about maximizing profit. It's about how you can learn to custom build a company for its competitive context. If you want to understand how to create one of those 100-year companies, read on.

6

CORPORATE IQ
Strategies for Success

Author's note. In the next three chapters, I will talk about the various aspects of Corporate IQ. In each chapter, I will discuss the concepts related to the seventeen areas of the company that comprise Corporate IQ. Toward the end of the book, I will provide a step-by-step explanation of how to apply each of the concepts practically. Once you've completed the book, you will be able to use Corporate IQ to enhance the performance of your organization and will have the practical tools to achieve that goal.

Smart companies are radical companies. I hope that message is coming through clearly. Smart companies rarely waste their resources to invest in seminars on the latest fad. They understand the basics that have made them successful, and one of those basics is their unwillingness to follow the crowd. Smart companies would rather lead than follow anyway. In many ways, the competitive roots of the smartest companies are iconoclastic in nature, and as long as that quality does not change, they will usually stay at the top of their industry.

It is important that you understand the extreme difference between how we have traditionally thought about corporate strategy and what I am proposing. The basic, yet extreme, difference between this methodology and all others is what I call "contextualization." In other words, rather than making our historic competencies, or our resources, the starting point for strategic planning, we begin with the context that the firm will face. Unless you are willing to begin with openness and an understanding of the firm's context, including the absolute requirement that the firm must match its competitive context, there is little hope for maximizing the future of the firm.

This is the missing link at the heart of competitive success: strategy must follow context. Motorola, Xerox, Kodak, and numerous others have proven that clearly. Sadly, they continue today to demonstrate what happens when the firm fails to fit context.

> Context-driven strategy is the missing link.

In Wharton's December 1, 2003, knowledge newsletter,[1] we see a chilling example of a company that has failed to maintain a fit with its context. The subtitle tells it all: "Does Sun, Burned by Competition, Need a New Business Model?" Notice the implicit issue that underlies the subtitle. Sun no longer fits its context. It has become the victim of creative destruction as competitors have changed their strategies for competing.

In my book *Thriving in E-Chaos,* I suggest that complexity impacts firms in a predictable manner, especially those that become inwardly focused and obsessed with their historic competencies. I call the process the "four-phase cycle of organizations." The less-than-smart companies generally start out like other companies, in a phase that I call "explosion." However, the firm's inability to fit its context soon leads to organizational stagnation. As the firm continues over time to reject the signals of change from the competitive environment, the firm goes into the crisis phase. Ultimately, the firm will cease to exist or go into the renewal phase. You will note that creative destruction as well as the impact of complexity are inextricably tied to each phase. In the case of Sun, the organization has clearly entered the late stages of stagnation (phase II) or the early stage of crisis (stage III).

BUILDING THE FOUNDATION: SMART COMPANIES

In the development of his original concept, H. Igor Ansoff hypothesized that the firm is made up of two broad areas. The first area, which he called strategic aggressiveness, involved the level of aggressiveness of the firm, both in marketing and innovation. In my research, I concluded that two additional areas of strategy needed to be considered: product portfolio balance and product technology applications. The second area Ansoff developed is called management responsiveness, or management capabilities, and has to do with the organization—its structure, culture, and other aspects that enable it to respond to environment-driven events.

When we think about it, Ansoff's ideas are analogous to sports. As a sailboat racer, I have to think about two issues at all times. First, can I use aggressive thrusts to put my competitor off balance? Second, my crew and I need to be capable of responding to uncertain events, such as a gust of wind or a competitor who tacks to try to put my boat in the wind shadow of his boat. It's all about the balancing of those two areas. I have to be thinking constantly about ways that I can attack my competitor, while at the same time be able to respond rapidly to attacks. Business is no different.

The company is able to engage in its own form of creative destruction by aggressively thrusting new products, new ideas, and marketing initiatives into the business environment. As I have said before, the marketplace of this century is one of continual creative destruction events. That, of course, is why a firm's "historic competencies" are usually irrelevant to the future. It is generally a waste of time to focus on what the firm used to do well instead of creating the firm's future. Again, it is important to remember that the company may be able to consider or extend some historic product areas, but it is suicidal for a manager to consider that strategy as the only possible future of the firm. More often than not, strategy is all about understanding what products we can commit to for the next year or so, what products we need to eliminate, and what we need to do to create an attractive future, regardless of whether or not we have supposed "competencies" in those areas. Let me put it another way: strategy is not about continuing the past; it's about creating the future.

> Strategy is not about continuing the past. It's about creating the future.

If a manager ever fails to realize that the *only* resource available is assets (not "resources"), the game may be over. By assets, I am referring to the dollars represented by those assets, not the resource that they represent. The only real competitive "resource" is cash. We have to think of assets in terms of cash—how they can be converted to cash—so that we can move to new areas of opportunity without regard to what we have done in the past. Just like the financial guru who gets rid of low-performing stocks in a portfolio, a good manager knows when to get rid of a declining stock to reinvest their funds in one with a future. This is what separates the good CEOs from the bad ones. Thinking out of the box means that you have to be willing to sacrifice your "core business" and supposed "competitive advantage" in favor of an opportunity to enhance radically the firm's future profit potential. If you are unwilling to do so, you don't need to be a CEO, because you are doing nothing less than putting your company at risk.

Again, it is important to revisit the idea of contextualization or, to put it another way, to recognize the need to custom build a company for its specific competitive environment. By now, it should be clear that the manager with the most accurate understanding of the external environment is usually the one who is able to best lead the company to maximum profitability. Let's begin our discussion on strategies by looking at the external environment from a systems thinking perspective. In Chapter 4, you learned that Ansoff developed a way of looking at the external environment that fit the systems thinking approach. Figure 6.1 shows the five levels of environmental turbulence that Ansoff developed.[2] It is important to remember that each level represents the combined effects of marketing and innovation turbulence.

In using this approach, it is possible to describe turbulence anywhere along the five-point scale. For example, turbulence of level 4.5 is a rapidly changing, complex (uncertain), highly competitive environment. In fact, at level 4.5, competition is nearly overwhelming. Here is the most important thing to remember about turbulence. Turbulence is nothing more than a description of your competitors' behavior or strategies. That is why I call turbulence the competitive index. It is a systems thinking index that describes the competitive environment with one number. Once you understand the competitive index for a segment, you also understand what the competitors in that segment will be doing as well as the effects of those strategies.

THE PROFIT ZONE

Now, I want to really ask you to think carefully about something. If the competitive index for an area is 4.0, what type of strategies do you think you need to deploy to be successful in that environment? The answer: level 4.0 strategies. Let me put it another way. If the firm's competitors will be highly innovative, aggressive, and extremely focused on increasing market share, can you do anything other than match that strategy if you want to survive? Of course the answer is no. You have no choice. The only problem you have is to figure out what a "level 4.0 strategy" is.

FIGURE 6.1   *The Effects of Turbulence*

1	2	3	4	5
Almost no competition	Negligible competition	Competitive	Highly competitive	Overwhelming competition
Little/no change	Moderate change	Fast change	Rapid change	Supersonic change
Long product life cycles	Extended PLCs	Moderate PLCs	Short PLCs	Extremely short PLCs
Low complexity; predictable	Moderate complexity	Complex but predictable	Highly complex unpredictable	Highly unpredictable and complex

Now that you know what a level 4.0 environment is, let's try to figure out how we might create a company that is custom designed for that environment. Consider Figure 6.2.

Now take a look at the company. Remember, the competitor index (level 4.0) reveals that the company's competition will be highly aggressive and, further, that the company will deal with a substantial amount of complexity and uncertainty. The profit zone—between 3.5 and 4.5—defines the range of profitable behavior for the firm. Notice that if the company's strategy was aggressive (level 3.0) and its competitors were operating at level 4.0, the company would be a consistent loser. Marketing and innovation at that level must consistently be ahead of the curve, and the firm must concentrate on growing (versus maintaining) market share. Notice as well that, if the firm decided to behave at level 5.0, it would be too aggressive for the competitive environment, spending much too much money and profit on marketing and innovation.

It's important to remember that the area of strategy includes four broad areas of the firm. This is a simple example but at the same time will hopefully help explain exactly how the profit zone works.

Notice as well that an organization profiled at level 1.0 would not do well in this environment at all. A steep, inflexible, internally focused organization will become extinct in such an environment. The organization will simply be unable to adapt to the discontinuities that are characteristic of a level 4.0 environment.

The final broad area of the firm is organizational character. Notice that there is only one standard for organizational character, and that is what I have called "unquestionable." Character includes ethics and value of subordinates. Organizational character must be of the highest level no matter

FIGURE 6.2   *Level 4.0 Strategy*

	1	2	3	4	5
Strategy	Slow follower	Follower	Aggressive	Very aggressive	Take no prisoners
Organization	Non-adaptive	Slow	Responsive	Adaptive	Highly adaptive
Character	Extremely	Low	Flexible	High	Unquestionable

what the competitive environment is doing. The years 2001 to 2003 have confirmed that reality as we watched the horror of the demise of Arthur Andersen, one of the world's largest accounting firms.

WHAT IS CORPORATE IQ?

Now that I have introduced the basic concept that underlies Corporate IQ, I would like to expand it. Figure 6.3 shows the 17 areas that make up Corporate IQ. Notice that each of the broad areas of strategy, organization, and character are further subdivided into distinct components.

I have no intention of continually picking on those who suggest that corporate strategy is little more than a weekend exercise for the board of directors, in which the firm's core competencies are determined from a SWOT analysis (strengths, weaknesses, opportunities, and threats) and the mission is then created to make sure the firm stays in the box. I do have a message for those who think that is what strategy is all about: Beware!

Smart managers and smart companies understand that each of the 17 areas of the firm are critical to long-term success. Companies like Luxottica (Lens Crafters and Sunglass Hut) and Southwest Airlines, to name just two of America's smartest companies, spend a great deal of time and effort managing each of the 17 areas.

In computing a company's Corporate IQ, I assess how a company is doing in each of the 17 areas. The closer to the profit zone that the company is operating in each area, the higher the firm's Corporate IQ. Yes, the research reveals that the higher the Corporate IQ, the higher the firm's profit. It's important to remember that we do not use the competitive index when it comes to organizational character: 5.0 is the only measure of character for a smart company. Smart leaders understand that the components of character, such as integrity or valuing subordinates, are the very foundation of any organization's success.

FIGURE 6.3   *The 17 Areas of Corporate IQ*

Strategy	Organization	Character
Marketing	CEO attributes	Values
Innovation	Managers	Ethics
Product-technology	Culture	Value of people
Product portfolio	Formal structure	Excellence rating
	Intelligence systems	Quality and process
	Corporate strategy	
	Attitude toward change	
	Internal technology applications	

You might be tempted to ask, "What if a firm is operating in its profit zone in 16 out of the 17 areas? Will that damage its profitability?" Numerous examples suggest that failing in even one area can substantially damage a firm's performance. In one case, I discovered a Fortune 100 company that was clearly operating in its profit zone in every area but one: marketing. In this case, the company was renowned for creating some of the most phenomenal, best-in-class products in the world. The only problem was, they were never able to reach their potential with their products because of their marketing deficiencies.

> Companies that operate out of their profit zone
> consistently snatch defeat from the jaws of victory.

With the basics under our belt, it's now time to look at the first major area of Corporate IQ—the firm's strategies. As I said before, strategy is the aggressive side of the firm. It's the engine that produces future profit potential. Absent great strategy work today, the firm has little hope for tomorrow.

ORGANIZATIONAL STRATEGY

In computing a firm's Corporate IQ, four areas of strategy are considered: marketing, innovation, product-technology applications, and the firm's product portfolio. In this chapter, each of those areas will be discussed. Notice that each of the 17 components of Corporate IQ are subdivided into a number of attributes.

This leads us to the area in which the Corporate IQ approach is radically different from all other approaches to corporate strategy. It begins with a systems thinking approach to determining competitor behavior called the competitive index. It then leads the manager to understand how to profile each area of the firm for that specific environment. Again, it's all about designing strategies and an organization for the specific competitive challenges that the firm will face. The bottom line: It's all about understanding how to keep the firm—every aspect of the firm—in the profit zone. The first area of strategy that we will consider is marketing aggressiveness.

I would again like to credit Igor Ansoff for his phenomenal work in creating not only his original strategic approach but, further, the entire process that allows a manager to look at a chart for each area of the firm and use that to understand how to design strategies. I cannot overemphasize the importance of what you are trying to achieve. On one hand, you have the competitive index, which describes expected competitor strategies. On the other, you can quickly assess your organization and identify deficiencies related to the profit zone in every area of the firm.

I would like to begin the discussion on strategy with a practical exercise. Let's assume that you are in the residential telecommunications business. It does not take long to figure out that the competitive index in that segment is around level 4.5. Now let's develop strategy based on that index.

Observe that I have indicated the competitor index in Figure 6.5 with the dotted vertical line at 4.5. Notice also, that I have drawn in the profit zone at +/- 0.5, which means that the profit zone for the firm is between 4.0 and 5.0. That means that if the firm's sales aggressiveness, PR/advertising aggressiveness, and market strategy is in that range, the firm will maximize its profitability. Remember also, the further away from the ideal (4.5), the lower the profit. I use the distance from the competitor index to arrive at the score, or IQ points, for each of the 17 areas of the firm.

Now I would like to add one more aspect to the chart. I would like to add a typical organizational profile to the chart, using small circles to indicate the firm's level of marketing aggressiveness. See Figure 6.6.

You can take one look at this profile and understand why this company will not be successful in the emerging market. While competitors will be highly aggressive, our firm will be a follower in the area of sales aggressiveness, will have negligible PR and marketing, and pay little attention to increasing market share. After seeing this exact situation in real companies numerous times, I can tell you that this company is all but dead.

This also helps explain why one of the fads like Six Sigma will not fix a problem-laden company. If you do not measure the right things, you cannot fix them. The answer is truly that simple, even though the process is com-

FIGURE 6.4 *Marketing (Aggressiveness)*

Factor	Level I	2	3	4	5
Sales aggressiveness	Low	Moderately low	Competitive	Moderately high	Highly aggressive
PR/Advertising aggressiveness	Negligible	Moderate	Competitive	Aggressive	Highly aggressive
Market strategy	Maintain market	Maintain market	Grow with market	Expand market	Increase market share

plex. I am not opposed to Six Sigma, by the way, but I do recognize that, while a Six Sigma program may be able to correct 10 percent of a company's problems, unless the other 90 percent are corrected, the firm will still fail. Six Sigma is only a fad if you view it as an all-consuming single solution.

The next area of strategy to consider is innovation aggressiveness. Notice again that, as the competitive index goes up, the creative activities of the firm must increase accordingly. In the area of customer focus, it is important to note that the long-accepted idea of "staying close to the customer" is an acceptable practice as long as the competitor index is level 3.0 or below. When the level of competitiveness exceeds 3.0, the firm must become proactively engaged in anticipating customer needs. That is another way of saying that the customer will often not know their own needs and will want to do business with the organization that can best provide solutions.

It is important to realize that innovation aggressiveness is the area of the firm that provides the fuel for the engine of profit. Without an appropriate level of innovation, the firm is not producing enough new products at an acceptable rate. Under those circumstances, the best marketing program in the world will not help.

FIGURE 6.5 *Marketing (Aggressiveness)*

Factor	Level I	2	3	4	5
Sales aggressiveness	Low	Moderately low	Competitive	Moderately high	Highly aggressive
PR/Advertising aggressiveness	Negligible	Moderate	Competitive	Aggressive	Highly aggressive
Market strategy	Maintain market	Maintain market	Grow with market	Expand market	Increase market share

FIGURE 6.6   *Marketing (Aggressiveness)*

Factor	Level I	2	3	4	5
Sales aggressiveness	Low	Moderately low	Competitive	Moderately high	Highly aggressive
PR/Advertising aggressiveness	Negligible	Moderate	Competitive	Aggressive	Highly aggressive
Market strategy	Maintain market	Maintain market	Grow with market	Expand market	Increase market share

As the level of competition or competitive index goes up, so must the levels of innovation and marketing aggressiveness. One way of measuring just how effectively a company is handling its innovation, or R&D program, is to look at its product life cycle balance.

Most companies tend to compete within a family of products. Technology companies tend to focus in a fairly narrow product area. I would like to add: this practice is not desirable; it is simply reality. People love to focus on the familiar and avoid the unfamiliar.

With that reality in mind, it is often also true that the competitive index for the various product segments will often be within the same range. That means that the product strategies across the company can be similar. One way that we can measure the effectiveness of a firm's innovation aggressiveness is to look at what I call the firm's product life cycle balance.

As the competitive index increases, product life cycles decrease. Think about it, as firms innovate more rapidly, events of creative destruction become more frequent. In turn, the useful sales life of a product will decrease. Here is what we normally expect to see at each different level of competition.

FIGURE 6.7   *Innovation (Aggressiveness)*

Factor	Level I	2	3	4	5
R&D spending	Low	Moderately low	Competitive	Moderately high	Highly aggressive
Product life cycles-plan	Very long	Long	Moderate	Short	Very short
Customer focus	Respond to demands	Meet demands	Stay close to customer	Anticipate needs	Anticipate unrealized needs

FIGURE 6.8   *The Competitive Index and Product Life Cycles*

Competitive Index	1	2	3	4	5
	7 years	5-7 years	5 years	3-5 years	18-36 months

I have not spent a great deal of time explaining how we derive the competitive index for a competitive segment. I also have not spent much time explaining why we normally measure the competitive index at some point in the future versus today. In a consulting situation, it takes about four to six weeks to complete the research required to accurately predict the future competitive index. The process is complex and somewhat sophisticated. Most importantly, it is extremely accurate. That's why some clients have chosen to retain our team solely for the purpose of computing the future competitor index for a segment. It helps them understand the most profitable product portfolio balance for the segment.

The final area of strategy is called product-technology (applications). In this area, many companies have learned some costly and important lessons over the past few years. Product-technology applications involves the inclusion of technology in products. One emerging technology that recently has had a significant impact on products and product marketing is the Internet. This particular aspect of the product can obviously take many forms, but needless to say, it is critically important and must be considered as part of any effective corporate strategic plan.

Technology clearly is the fuel that drives the future of a company. One of the best known technology companies is Microsoft, which is one of the ten smartest companies in America.

FIGURE 6.9   *The Four Stages of Products (Life Cycle)*

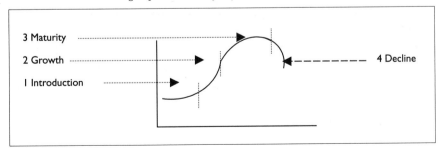

FIGURE 6.10   *Product Portfolio*

Factor	Level 1	2	3	4	5
Diversification (Product)	None	Limited	Moderate	High	Very high
Product life cycle balance	Mostly 3-4	Mostly 3-4	Balance (1-4)	Skewed toward 1-3	Skewed toward 1-2

MICROSOFT: ONE OF THE TOP TEN SMARTEST COMPANIES IN AMERICA

When it comes to identifying great companies, Microsoft is on just about every list. In the case of this book, it made the list because the internal assessment of the firm indicated that they are a very smart company. At the same time, a lot of people try to find something wrong with the company. Regardless, the unavoidable truth is that Microsoft has exceptional strategy, a highly adaptive organization, and exceptional corporate character. It's hard to be critical of such a well-run company.

Microsoft, it turns out, is run a lot like the other smart companies featured in this book. A few years ago, I had the opportunity to interview employee number 1,500 of Microsoft. It is clear that the company is run exactly the same way today as it was in those early years. Bill Gates still seeks excellence from himself and from everyone else associated with the company. He is still the resident visionary and is obsessed with discovering the future first.

One of the ways that Microsoft has maintained its growth and profitability is through its focus on intellectual capital and knowledge. The organization begins with hiring the best, most talented people. They also make sure that the people they hire will fit the Microsoft culture as well as the company's attitude toward excellence. One of the mantras of Bill Gates is the need to share knowledge within the company. In the early years, he made it clear that a discovery such as a new trend or process in one part of the company had to be shared immediately across the organization. That is where those smart, capable people come in. As superb as Microsoft is as a learning organization, they are probably equally adept at applying organizational learning in the form of implementation.

Great people, aggressive strategy, continual learning, and exceptional corporate character: Microsoft is one of those exceptionally smart companies that should continue to do well over time.

FIGURE 6.11   *Technology Applications (Product)*

Factor	Level 1	2	3	4	5
Technology applications (Product)	None	Limited	Moderate	High	Very high
Technology philosophy	None	Last In	Adapt with competition	Seek early adaptation	First mover

STRATEGY FOLLOWS CONTEXT

Great companies are adept not only at creating great products on a continual basis but at marketing them. Smart leaders and smart companies have the foresight to spend money on innovation, even in hard times, because that is how they create the future. At the top ten smartest companies, each clearly can continually create strategies that are appropriate for the firm's context. If you look out into the world of commerce, the same cannot be said for a lot of companies. At those companies, it takes a crisis to convince the firm's management of a strategy problem. Often, that realization occurs much too late.

Author comments. I have based my research on the original work of H. Igor Ansoff. While I have extensively modified his original model, I credit him for creating the first comprehensive model of the environment as well as the organization. I will forever be indebted to Dr. Ansoff for his insightful teaching and mentoring.

7

ORGANIZATION

Entrepreneurial Support Systems

Ever wonder why some great emerging companies did not last very long? Have you ever seen a company that had a great product but was unable to operate at a level sufficient to get the results that it deserved? If you have seen companies like that, and most of us have, this chapter will hopefully provide a lot of answers for you. I'll begin by telling you a true story. I have changed only the name to protect the guilty.

ZEUS ELECTRONICS

Zeus Electronics is not a small company. In fact, it ranks well toward the top of one of the major top 100 lists. What makes Zeus unique is a business combination that occurred just a few short years ago. One of the firms involved in the consolidation has its roots in the early 1900s. The other was over a half a century old at the time of the consolidation. One company had reached the point of being a high Corporate IQ firm. The other had a Corporate IQ of around 50—one of the lowest scores that I have ever seen. Sadly, the low-IQ company ended up on top after the consolidation.

What followed was a systematic destruction of the acquired firm's leadership structure as well as its culture. Within a few short years, empowering managers had been replaced by highly controlling managers. The culture of excellence became a culture of compliance. Soon, the exodus of talented, creative members of the corporate team left the firm with a slow, bureaucratic group with little ability or desire to engage in creativity. The organization had lost its ability to be innovative or responsive.

Since the consolidation, the firm has laid off tens of thousands of workers. Finally, they were able to lay off enough workers to squeeze out a profit. The promotional policies at the firm clearly favored those from the firm that came out on top. One employee, in talking about the firm's new promotional policies, put it this way: "If you fail the IQ test, you get promoted."

At first, I really could not believe some of the stories that I was hearing about this company. However, after confirming them with about ten different sources, I concluded that they must be true.

UNDERSTANDING CORE INTELLIGENCE

While some worry about a firm's core competencies, I worry a lot more about a firm's core intelligence. A few years ago, I did an external study of Apple Computer, just before Steve Jobs returned to run the company. Years of bureaucratic management and repressive dealings had led to a massive exodus from the company. Repressive bureaucracies do not cause the slugs to leave the company—the slugs don't have anyplace to go. Repressive bureaucracies cause the people who can leave—the bright, talented ones—to leave. The situation is a classic brain drain.

Some have claimed recently that their research shows that a firm's CEO is somewhat irrelevant to its sustainability. I would have to say that I disagree with that conclusion for a number of reasons. First, the anecdotal evidence is that the CEO does matter. Problem companies change for the better when a strong, knowledgeable CEO comes in. In the same way, we can observe numerous instances in which a high-performing company starts a downward trend when a new CEO arrives. Second, the research underlying Corporate IQ simply does not support their hypothesis. With that in mind, let's begin looking at the various aspects of the organization.

Before looking at specific areas, it is probably a good idea to revisit the Corporate IQ model. The approach measures three broad areas of the organization.

1. Strategy (the aggressiveness factors)
2. Organization (the adaptive factors)
3. Character (the sustainability factors)

FIGURE 7.1 *CEO Attributes*

Factor	Level 1	2	3	4	5
Attitude toward change	Reject	Resist	Slow adaption	Drive change	Aggressively drive change
Attitude toward creativity and risk	No value	Devalue	Necessary evil	Drive creativity	Aggressively Promote
Attitude toward subordinates	Expect performance	Expect efficiency	Meet objectives	Respect and value	Encourage as team member

Also, it is important to remember that the profit zone for character never varies; it is always at level 5.0. In the case of strategy and organization, those areas are context dependent. In other words, the profit zone can move along the scale from 1.0 to 5.0. Success is all about contextualization and matching the company with its context.

CEO ATTRIBUTES

CEO attributes really involves all the other 16 broad areas of the firm. I put it in the organization area because it seems to fit best there. That said, let us take a look at the attributes of the CEO that are important to organizational success (see Figure 7.1).

In many areas that are measured using the Corporate IQ approach, positioning an aspect of the organization such as "advertising and public relations aggressiveness" out of the profit zone on the high side will cost the company money. In a few areas, such as "attitude toward subordinates," that is not true. Even if the competitive index is in the 2.0 to 3.0 range (uncompetitive), valuing subordinates will increase profitability. Therefore, the profit zone minimums obviously are more important than the maximums in some areas.

Let us assume for a moment that you were on the board of a company like Motorola. (In 2003, Motorola's chairman Chris Galvin indicated his intention to leave the post.) Let us also assume that Motorola's environment or competitive index (its context) is generally in the level 4.3 range. What type of CEO does Motorola need? (See Figure 7.2)

It is fairly common knowledge that, when Galvin announced his intentions, Motorola had become a restrictive bureaucracy. There were still pockets of innovation within the firm, but getting a good idea to market is still a problem.

FIGURE 7.2 *Desired CEO/Chairman Attributes: Motorola*

Factor	Level 1	2	3	4	5
Attitude toward change	Reject	Resist	Slow adaption	Drive change	Aggressively drive change
Attitude toward creativity and risk	No value	Devalue	Necessary evil	Drive creativity	Aggressively Promote
Attitude toward subordinates	Expect performance	Expect efficiency	Meet objectives	Respect and value	Encourage as team member

Finding the CEO/chairman that Motorola needs may prove a difficult task. In a lot of cases, CEOs like to build control structures and establish their own little bureaucracy. That would obviously be a major mistake for Motorola. What the company needs is someone to shake its foundations. In some ways, it needs to get back to its entrepreneurial roots. Rather than establishing a new bureaucracy, the new CEO will need to come in with a "challenge everything" attitude. Obviously, the existing management team could prove to be the biggest challenge for the new head.

While I disagreed with a few things that Carly Fiorina did when she became Hewlitt-Packard's new CEO, I really admire her for creating a few simple rules to establish a new way of doing business. Here are the three rules that she instituted when she came in the door.

Carly **F**iorina's **T**hree **R**ules

1. Preserve the best, reinvent the rest.
2. No politics, no bureaucracy.
3. Radical ideas are not bad ideas.[1]

The enormous task that Motorola's new CEO will face is immediately obvious. Not only is there an immediate need to reinvent much of the firm, but there is strong internal resistance. The wisdom of the board of directors will have an enormous impact on the future of the firm. Yes, CEOs really do matter.

ORGANIZATIONAL MANAGEMENT

When you walk into a company, a bit of attention to detail can tell you an awful lot. Regardless of what they tell you, most companies have a very clear philosophy of management. That philosophy usually plays out in two areas: leadership style and risk propensity. One area that I will discuss in depth in a later chapter is control and controlling managers. At many 100-year companies that have been featured by the likes of Jim Collins, it is not surprising to find a highly controlling leadership style as a common philosophy in the firm. Because most of those companies are competing in segments where the competitive index is over level 4.0, a control-oriented philosophy clearly makes little sense.

"But these are those renowned, 100-year companies," you might say. I would respond and recognize the accomplishment of the company's ability to sustain itself for 100 years. As I have investigated such companies, what I have discovered is that they do a lot of things well. In the case of GE, they have a product portfolio approach that enables the firm to revitalize its product mix continually and even make radically different investments (a real no-no in some management circles) to sustain growth.

With all of that said, these companies are still operating with level 3.0 management practices in segments with competitive indexes in excess of 4.0. I would like to make two important points that relate to this issue. First, most of these 100-year companies are tied to demand cycles of over 100 years. They did not start out life in the hula hoop segment. They started the corporate life in a segment with a demand cycle in excess of 100 years. It was not planned; it just happened. Second, and most importantly: sustainability is not necessarily a measure of management excellence. I would fully expect a 100-year-old sugar company to continue to be around for at least another 50 years. The reason is simply that the commodity called sugar will be in demand for the next 50 years, at least. Sustainability in cases where the company is tied to a 100-year demand cycle does not indicate organizational excellence.

I have had the opportunity to work with and study some of the companies I am talking about. Across the board, I have concluded that if the leadership style of those firms were changed from a disciplined, goal-oriented approach (level 3.0) to that of empowered excellence (level 4.0), the ROI of those firms would go up substantially. In other words, they are doing well because of their circumstances, but in every case they could do a lot better.

FIGURE 7.3 *Management (Organizational)*

Factor	Level 1	2	3	4	5
Leadership style	Controlling	Moderately controlling	Results oriented	Empowering	Inspirational
Attitude toward risk	Reject	Discourage	Tolerate	Encourage	Expect

If the CEO is the cornerstone of an organization, then the leadership philosophy is the foundation. As you will discover in Chapter 10, leadership not only establishes the context for innovation but also fosters adaptive behavior. Both are critical for firms operating in segments with competitive indexes above level 4.0, over 90 percent of the companies in the world.

CORPORATE CULTURE

I hope you are carefully reading each of the charts on the 17 areas. Most of us have worked for a company with a level 1.0 culture at some point in our lives. An organizational culture that focuses on "defending the status quo, devaluing employees, and rewarding historic performance" is usually a revolving door. The literature talks about adaptive and nonadaptive cultures. It should surprise no one to discover that most troubled companies have a level 1.0 or 2.0 culture. That makes a lot of sense, because most of the time, the complexity of the environment deals the organization numerous surprises and challenges. By definition, a nonadaptive culture destroys a firm's ability to deal with such discontinuities.

A PAUSE FOR SOME MUSIC

A number of times in this book, I will revisit an analogy that I frequently use to reinforce the concept of an organization as a complex system. A company is much like an orchestra. If one part of the orchestra is out of sync, the music stinks. I can attest to that reality personally, because I spent much of my youth playing in high school and college orchestras. All it takes is one instrument or one section of an orchestra to be out of sync with the rest of the group, and the music really does stink. The same is true for a company.

FIGURE 7.4 *Culture*

Factor	Level 1	2	3	4	5
Values	Defend the status quo	Support the status quo	Maintain the status quo	Challenge status quo	Create the future
Value of employees	Little	Minimal	Moderate	High	Very high
Rewards and incentives	Historic performance	Accuracy and efficiency	Productivity	Solutions development	Creativity

Notice the interdependence between CEO attributes, organizational management, and corporate culture. Each is dependent on the other. Bring in a control freak CEO, for example, and you will destroy the firm's culture and diminish the level of organizational management.

Also, consider the impact of the CEO, management, and culture on the company's innovation efforts. A risk-averse, control-oriented philosophy can quickly destroy the ability of the firm to use its core intelligence.

ORGANIZATIONAL STRUCTURE

In the same way that the literature talks about adaptive and nonadaptive cultures, it talks about flexible and inflexible structures. Stop for a moment and consider the logic that underlies Corporate IQ. It makes a lot of sense to have an adaptive culture in a highly complex, uncertain environment. It also makes a lot of sense to have a flexible structure in that environment. That is why most people who look at Corporate IQ ultimately say that it is simply a matter of logic. That is true of an organization's structure. Structure is simply a description of how the people and functions in an organization are connected. It would be logical to assume that the more complex the firm's context, the more complex the firm's structure should be.

It is also pretty obvious that a steep bureaucracy will kill a firm when the competitive index exceeds level 3.5. The question is, what types of structures are appropriate for each level? Figure 7.5 helps us understand that.

One of the concepts that Ansoff created is the bicentralized power structure. A matrix structure (level 4.0) is one in which there is connectivity not only to a functional area but also to a product area (or some variation of that idea). Figure 7.6 shows a simplistic matrix structure.

FIGURE 7.5 *Structure*

Factor	Level 1	2	3	4	5
Formal structure	Hierarchy	Functional	Divisional	Matrix	Matrix
Power focus	Senior executive	Bureaucracy	Executive and bureaucracy	Distributed CEO/team	Bicentralized*

*A bicentralized focus on power involves a high level of creative leadership at the top and highly empowered teams at the competitive level.

You will note that in a matrix structure, each member of the team has two reporting relationships. First, each has the normal function responsibility. Second, each also serves as part of a product team. One of the benefits of the matrix structure is the fact that it cuts out a lot of the politics associated with decisions. Because each functional area has direct participation in every product, the product gets good representation in the functional area. That fact alone can help most organizations.

DECISION SYSTEMS

There has been a lot of talk over the past few years about intellectual capital. What exactly is intellectual capital? Intellectual capital might best be characterized as knowledge that reveals the optimal future path of the organization. The real issue involves both organizational learning as well as speed of decisions.

I know I have suggested numerous times that management is all about philosophy. That is especially clear when you think about organizational learning. Most companies gather the same data. Why, then, does one company use that data to create a wonderful future, while its competitor ignores the information and goes into a downward spiral? It is all founded on that elusive concept called organizational learning.

Organizational learning has to do with the ability of organizational members to convert data to knowledge, then to act upon that knowledge. Knowledge contains intellectual capital. It is the intellectual capital, be it a business process, a new customer preference, or a patent, that becomes the future profit of a firm. Intellectual capital resides in a firm's people. It is not something you can put in a fireproof vault. That explains the inevitable revenue tumble that firms with restrictive bureaucracies experience when

FIGURE 7.6   *A Typical Matrix Structure*

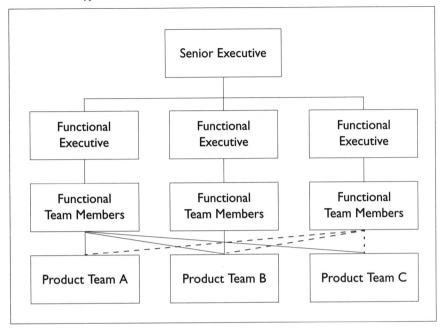

their intellectual capital walks out the door in protest of treatment by senior executives.

When we look at decision systems, we are concerned first with how data is collected. Obviously, the higher the expected competitive index, the more futuristic the nature of the intelligence that must be gathered. Pair that with a commitment to high-speed decision making, and you have an organization that can compete at supersonic speeds.

I would like to point out that most organizations do not have an intelligence unit. Most that do have an intelligence unit tend to be market intelligence focused. Often, the intelligence unit operates under the sales department. Intelligence units need to report directly to the CEO to be successful. Further, intelligence personnel not only need to be equipped with the latest data capabilities, but they further need access to the latest analysis tools. In many cases, intelligence personnel are taught how to do a SWOT analysis (strengths, weaknesses, opportunities, and threats) on a competitor, plus a Porter's Five Forces Industry Analysis, and little more. As intelligence tools, these approaches are severely limited, because they lack the predictive power required for complex, high-speed environments.

FIGURE 7.7 *Decision Systems*

Factor	Level 1	2	3	4	5
Speed of decisions	Very slow	Slow	Moderate	Fast	Extremely fast
Early warning systems	None	Limited	Competitive intelligence	Strategic intelligence	Multiple systems

INTERNAL TECHNOLOGY APPLICATIONS

The ability to support high levels of strategic aggressiveness as well as foster speed-of-light adaptive behavior depends upon the internal technology of the firm. It is often easy to justify cutting the technology budget in highly competitive times, because profit is so hard to achieve in those environments. More often than not, however, the failure to invest in appropriate technologies will haunt a company for years to come. The evidence, although anecdotal, is everywhere.

STRATEGIC PLANNING

Strategic planning can help, or destroy, a company. By now, you realize that I believe that strategic planning, as most companies practice it, keeps them well below their profit potential. In some cases, I suspect that it can destroy companies. If you question that reality, just look around and ask yourself why certain companies fail. In most cases, it gets down to flawed strategy. Generally, the environment has changed, but the firm has not.

FIGURE 7.8 *Technology Applications (Internal)*

Factor	Level 1	2	3	4	5
Technology strategy	Very slow adaptation	Slow adaptation	Stay with competition	Leading edge, not bleeding edge	Consistent first mover
Redundancy*	Unnecessary	Unimportant	Important	Serious	Critical

*Redundancy refers to the value placed upon the ability to take over for an operating system. It is assumed that all systems are backed up, but the firm could not stay in operation if the system were to go down. Obviously, some systems must be redundant regardless of the turbulence of the environment (health, safety, etc.)

FIGURE 7.9   *Strategic Planning*

Factor	Level I	2	3	4	5
Planning model	Budgeting	Business Analysis	Competency based*	Nonlinear**	Nonlinear
Planning technology	Manual	Computer projections	Complex budgeting	Artificial intelligence	Artificial intelligence

*The competency-based or traditional strategic model is based upon historic core competencies, competitive advantage, and mission.
**Corporate IQ is a comprehensive, nonlinear strategic planning approach.

Notice that the competency-based approach appears to work up to a level 3.0 competitive index. I said *appears* for a reason. When the competitive index is below 3.0, we know that change is fast, but the environment is still predictable. With that in mind, the approach will at least appear to work in such environments.

STRATEGIC CAPACITY

As the level of complexity in a competitive segment increases, so does the level of uncertainty. With that in mind, it becomes important for staff and executives alike to be capable of doing creative strategic work. There is little sense in creating a bicentralized power structure without giving the entire team the tools with which to make decisions about complex situations.

Some of the tools that can be used are complex systems thinking (or systems thinking), scenarios, and war gaming. In the case of all three, they clearly are designed to help the manager think through the multiple possibilities of any situation. Earlier, I suggested that the whole idea behind systems thinking is to make reliable inferences. It is not only possible to make reliable inferences about complex futures, but even in situations where it is not, the very fact that you understand the level of uncertainty can help you craft an appropriate strategy for the situation.

FIGURE 7.10   *Strategic Capacity*

Factor	Level I	2	3	4	5
Senior executive team	Very low	Low	Moderate	High	Very high
Staff/Managers	Very low	Low	Moderate	High	Very high

The difficulty in getting senior staff to think in terms of difference cannot be understated. It is a real challenge, because the power basis from which most executives operate is tied up in the old paradigm. Moving to a new paradigm of necessity involves leaving a personal power base behind and learning to think in new terms. Research has demonstrated that it is an extremely difficult change for an individual to make.

One company with a consistent record in creating a sustainable organization is Fidelity Investments. Fidelity is one of the top ten smartest companies in America.

FIDELITY INVESTMENTS: ONE OF THE TOP TEN SMARTEST COMPANIES IN AMERICA

Fidelity Investments is well known for its array of mutual funds and the services it provides to its customers. At Fidelity, the real story is what you don't see. It's a dynamic organization that is continually challenging every assumption about the future.

As with the other top ten smartest companies, Fidelity is keenly aware of how employees impact corporate performance. The firm's leadership knows well that "how you treat your people is how they treat your customers."

While writing this book, I was interviewed by an author who was writing a magazine article on productivity. One of the main questions she had was about productivity departments. "Do any of your top companies have productivity departments?" she asked. I explained that they did not but rather that productivity was a result of what I call "empowered excellence." I went on to explain that, at the top ten smartest companies, productivity was built into their culture in the form of excellence. That is excellence in how their people were treated and excellence in everything that every member of the team did. Excellence translates into productivity. That is exactly what and how Fidelity leads its people.

Another little-known fact about Fidelity is extremely important. Behind the scenes, Fidelity is a technology innovator. They have entire teams that work on creating the next technology application to serve their massive customer base. Their national networks are not only redundant but linked such that every customer transaction is simultaneously mirrored at all of the firm's technology centers.

Obviously, technology plays an important role in the development of the firm's overall strategy. They also spend a great deal of time in recognizing, appreciating, and valuing employees. The result is a highly adaptive organization that is founded on the highest standards of organizational character.

MAXIMIZING THE ADAPTIVE BEHAVIORS OF THE ORGANIZATION

Research shows a direct correlation between the age of an organization and the aggressive as well as the adaptive abilities of a firm. As organizations age, they tend to become inflexible and inwardly focused.

The ability to keep the firm's strategies operating in the profit zone is totally dependent upon the organization. Just like that orchestra, each piece of the puzzle must fit the competitive context. As a manager, you have the opportunity to make a significant difference in the future of your organization. Now, you have the foundation from which to launch just such an initiative.

Author comments. I have based my research on the original work of H. Igor Ansoff. While I have extensively modified his original model, I credit him for creating the first comprehensive model of the environment as well as the organization. I will forever be indebted to Dr. Ansoff for his insightful teaching and mentoring.

CHARACTER

The Sustainability Factor

The corporate meltdowns of the early 2000s produced a new emphasis on corporate and individual ethics. Many changes have resulted. There are new standards for corporate governance as well as changes in accounting and reporting standards. While these changes are welcome, the manager should remember that character is not the process of complying with external laws and regulations. Character is in establishing the very soul of the company. Further, character is much more than ethics or compliance. Character involves the values of the organization—its ethics, value of people, attitude toward excellence, and its attitude toward quality as well as process.

One of the first observations you will make about transformational leaders, those who take organizations to new highs, is that they often spend a great deal of time in the areas that I have listed as organizational character. One problem, according to many who comment on leadership issues, is the link that exists between a transformational leader and the organization. In a number of cases, when the transformational leader departs a company, performance suffers because the foundation or link with the character attributes is gone. I agree: transformational leaders are exceptional people, but it is critically important for character attributes to be tied to the firm itself instead of to the personality of a charismatic leader. Smart leaders understand that and make every effort to ingrain organizational character into the firm itself. Corporate character is comprised of five broad areas.

1. Values
2. Ethics
3. Value of people
4. Excellence
5. Quality and process

Every one of those areas drives the sustainability of the firm. In a world where the rules of the game change constantly, some character issues should never change.

Some organizations encourage storytelling to keep the emphasis on character at the forefront. At Mary Kay Inc., Mary Kay herself oversaw the creation of a "heritage department" that had the responsibility of recording and communicating the rich stories that have characterized that company over the years.

The literature on leadership talks about the role of leaders in providing meaning to various aspects of an organization. Leaders often use ceremony and recognition to emphasize and give meaning to important aspects of corporate character. They also go out of their way to walk the talk in areas that involve character. From her firm's founding moment, Mary Kay Ash spent much of her time building the foundation of the organization's character. If one of the hundreds of thousands of beauty consultants had a family tragedy, it was not unusual for Mary Kay to hear about it and call the individual, even to continue to follow up with the individual for an extended period of time. As a result of spending her time establishing the meanings behind the corporate focus, the emphasis on character continued after she became disabled in the late 1990s.

The events of 9/11 had an impact on the Mary Kay organization. A number of Mary Kay Inc. consultants lost their lives in that tragedy. A visit with a Mary Kay executive will reveal that they are still keeping in touch today with those impacted by 9/11. Living the principle of "the value of people" takes precedence in the lives of those at the top of the organization. That is how smart leaders at smart companies live their lives. They give meaning to the character issues of the firm by giving them priority in their own lives. They simply demonstrate by doing.

FIGURE 8.2 *Ethics*

	1	2	3	4	5
Policies	Non-existent	Hazy	Situational	Clear standards	Unquestionable standards
Support	None	Marginal	Moderate	Strong	Uncompromising

terminated." Obviously, the company that consistently promotes the best person for the job will be the most profitable, as well as a diverse, organization. It just makes sense.

The second area of ethics has to do with what I call support. Support deals with the level of compliance that exists within the company in the ethics area. A lot of people talk about ethics; a few take action. The issue is simply how strongly the firm's ethical standards are supported within the firm, top to bottom.

I know it may seem a bit ridiculous to measure something like this, but my experience has been that numerous problems with ethical standards and support exist within organizations. I am sure that Enron and Arthur Andersen had great-sounding ethical statements. The problem is, the standards must be exact and the support must be uncompromising at all levels of the firm. Otherwise, the firm has no ethical standards.

VALUE OF PEOPLE

Chapter 9 is devoted entirely to this topic. In some ways, value of people could be considered a part of the firm's culture. Most importantly, it is a critical part of the firm's profit strategy. Value of people refers to how the organization does business. It refers to the very core of every interpersonal transaction that occurs within an organization.

It should surprise no one that the turnover for a level 1 firm (abuse employees) is exponentially higher than a level 5 firm (exceptional). That also explains why many of the "best to work for" companies have the most talented people and also often enjoy higher earnings.

We also know that how employees are treated has a significant impact in other areas. For example, at one company, where supervisors were told they would be accountable for how they treated their subordinates, customer satisfaction, employee satisfaction, and unit performance all went up. W. Edwards Deming once said, "What gets measured gets done." It turns out that

FIGURE 8.3 *Value of People*

	1	2	3	4	5
Value of People	Abuse	Discount	Tolerate	Appreciate	Exceptional

if we make managers accountable for how people are valued, it happens. The results can be exceptional.

EXCELLENCE RATING

Excellence is an attitude. Although the idea has been criticized, there is a place for an appropriate standard of excellence. In many of the popular business books of the last 20 years, the theme has been excellence. The only problem with those writings is the vague nature of their definition of *excellence*. Most of the books tried to look at companies that happened to be doing well at the time. In almost every case, the authors tried to identify the keys of excellence that related to the firm's performance.

In most cases, the excellence books are mostly about practices. Sometimes, they involve what might be called best practices, as does the scorecard approach. The common problem of those books is context. They do not reveal the relationship between practice and context.

Excellence in its purest form is simply a definition or standard. Excellence has nothing to do with best practices or anything else that someone is doing. Excellence has to do with establishing an outrageous performance goal. Excellence can deal with how employees are treated, how customers are treated, or the new products that the company will create. Excellence simply has to do with setting the highest of all possible goals.

When applying the excellence rating to product innovation, the rating begins to make sense. What do the smartest and greatest companies do differently from their counterparts? The answer: They break the mold. While their competitors are busily benchmarking the work of others, the smart companies are trying to figure out how to establish a new standard. Profitability is all about changing the rules of the game, and every member of the corporate team must be committed to excellence.

FIGURE 8.4 *Excellence Rating*

	1	2	3	4	5
Excellence rating	Non-existent	Very low	Low	High	Exceptional

QUALITY AND PROCESS

You might wonder why I would include the ideas of quality and process after I just slammed things like benchmarking and best practices. I want to tell you two things. One, smart companies understand that quality is the competitive minimum. Second, smart companies continually question and revise their processes.

Smart companies understand that quality is a minimum. It's not a question, and it's also not a program. Quality is simply a way of life as well as an organizational commitment at smart companies.

The issue of process is equally important. A lot of consulting firms passed themselves off as process reengineering specialists, when in actuality they were little more than downsizing experts. Process has to do with cycle times, such as how long it takes from when an order is placed until it is shipped. At smart companies, every member of the team is a consultant. Everyone can question the process, and if there is a way to get a product to a customer faster, the entire organization will support the change. An openness to process change is a way of life at smart companies. One of the companies that is known for its corporate character is A.G. Edwards, one of the ten smartest companies in America.

A.G. EDWARDS: ONE OF THE TEN SMARTEST COMPANIES IN AMERICA

Want to know the name of the securities firm that did not go in the tank during the crash of 1929? Are you interested in finding out about the company that has made the "best to work for" list nine times? If you are, I need to tell you about A.G. Edwards.

A.G. Edwards is over 100 years old. Even after all of that time, the company is one of those rare organizations that thinks and acts out of the box. Headquartered in St. Louis, Missouri, A.G. Edwards has avoided some of the herd mentality pitfalls that others in the securities business have encoun-

FIGURE 8.5 *Quality and Process*

	1	2	3	4	5
Quality	No standard	Little focus	TQM programs	A way of life	A total Commitment
Process	Unchangeable	Inflexible	Resist change	Change as necessary	Continual revision

tered. "We think being out of New York is a positive for us," said one executive. "It helps us keep our focus on the customer instead of all the 'hot tips' that are so tempting for a lot of people." The executive went on to say that the company has a unique organization. Everything focuses on the customer and the financial consultant. All products and offerings relate to them.

This approach would be considered unusual for many in the industry. At some firms, the brokers are given quotas of specific securities that they must sell. "We don't allow that," said the executive. She continued, "Our financial consultants are expected to avoid such deals and do only what is in the best interest of their customers. We are here to provide support for them in achieving those goals. We view anything else as a conflict of interest,"

Old firm or not, A.G. Edwards has the aggressive strategies and the highly responsive organization that is easily capable of succeeding on a long-term basis. The firm also spends a great deal of time making sure that the character standards, like ethics, are exceptionally high.

One way that the company maintains its ability to remain above reproach in dealing with employees and customers is through its monthly call-in broadcast over the corporate network. Bob Bagby, CEO, conducts the sessions, and any employee of the firm can call and ask a question or complain. The employees may remain anonymous. Bagby welcomes any and all calls, because he believes that way the company can maintain the highest standards of customer service.

At smart companies, walking the talk is critically important. Integrity and valuing employees create an environment of trust that carries over to the customer. That's how business is done at A.G. Edwards, truly one of the smartest companies in America.

SMART COMPANIES AND CHARACTER

We have witnessed the demise of some companies that had great strategy and even a few that had a highly adaptive organization. The bottom line of sustainability is that it takes all three: aggressive strategy, an adaptive organization, and unquestionable character.

Companies really are analogous to an orchestra. The weakest performer can cause a disastrous performance. In some ways, it is difficult for a smart company to fail. Their strategy keeps them ahead of competitors, their adaptive abilities allow them to respond effectively to uncertainty and surprises, and their character allows them to sustain the first two.

Author comments. I have based my research on the original work of H. Igor Ansoff. While I have extensively modified his original model, I credit him for creating the first comprehensive model of the environment as well as the organization. I will forever be indebted to Dr. Ansoff for his insightful teaching and mentoring.

9

THE ULTIMATE MOTIVATOR

As a manager, you have a choice. You can pay someone exactly the same money for the same job as your competitor and get half as much productivity. Or you can pay them exactly the same money and get twice the productivity. It is your choice. Contrary to popular opinion, money is not a motivator. If you think that it is the ultimate motivator, it is time to rethink. If what I am saying is true, you might get only 50 percent of the effort from an employee that your competitor gets from an equally qualified individual who is paid the same. So, what is the difference?

The answer is "significance." In the field of psychology, the idea of significance has begun to emerge as a major theory of motivation. The idea of significance is somewhat simple. If you find a way to communicate that you believe another is significant, chances are that they will be motivated by your view. Let me put it another way: if you recognize your employees as significant, chances are that your company will be much more profitable than a competitor who does not recognize the significance of their employees.

In our book, *The Significance Principle,* Dr. Les Carter and I devote a lot of time to that concept. Les believes that the human desire to be recognized by others is one of the most powerful motivators in the makeup of the human being. I agree. When we look at people who want to run for political office or become a senior executive of a company, more often than not their drive is all about significance. The bottom line is that we spend a great deal of time and effort with the sole objective of being significant.

What if you worked at a company where one of the base values was to recognize the value of people? What do you think the bottom line of that company would be versus that of its nonsignificance-focused competitor? Undoubtedly, the company that focused on the value of its people would be much more profitable than its counterpart.

Let me stop for a moment. I have seen companies that forgot about the customer, the future, and excellence that have ended up in the dumps, even though they spent a great deal of effort on communicating the significance of their employees. There is a saying: beauty may be skin deep, but ugly goes clean to the bone. The same is true of ego and stupidity. When a company fails to manage all of the factors that drive profit (the 17 areas that comprise Corporate IQ), then I would expect the firm to enter the stagnation or crisis phase. That said, if a company is doing everything else well but its managers fail to recognize the significance of the entire team, the firm will not be a top performer in its segment.

One might ask: "What about GE? They are not known for valuing their people, yet they have been featured as one of those top companies in a lot of business books." My response is simple: GE is probably underperforming. In spite of their results, they are leaving a lot of money on the table. I'll explain further.

An acquaintance was recently offered a job with GE. The contract involved a very high salary, but one of the conditions of the job concerned her a lot. They wanted her to leave home on Sunday and not return until Saturday morning, just to make sure she maximized her customer contact time Monday through Friday. She is a bright individual, so it should not surprise you that she quickly figured out that she would not be appreciated as an individual. It was one of those impersonal, "perform or else" situations. She accepted a position at another major firm and immediately became one of their top performers. Her bottom line was simply that she wanted to work at a company where she was appreciated as an individual, not just for her performance. In that case, GE missed hiring an individual who could have made a serious contribution to their bottom line.

At a lot of companies, compliance is much more important than performance. Yes, companies with an "Attila the Hun" attitude about making the numbers can do fairly well, but at the same time, they leave a substantial amount of profit on the table. People live to be appreciated and valued. It is why they get up in the morning. Extremely bright and capable people will work for lower wages if their employer communicates their significance. It's important!

I must tell you that all of the top ten smartest companies in America focus on the issue of significance. It was difficult to choose which of those companies might be the most representative of that attitude. In the end, I had to focus on Mary Kay Inc., and the company's founder, Mary Kay Ash. Of all of the executives who have ever led a company, Mary Kay understood the value of significance. I had the opportunity to interview David Holl, CEO of the company. As you read his comments, I think you will understand just how important significance is at that company and why they have enjoyed double-digit growth every year since their founding in 1963.

MARY KAY INC.: ONE OF THE TOP TEN SMARTEST COMPANIES IN AMERICA

"Integrity, intelligence, energy: it all starts at the top," says Mary Kay Inc.'s president and COO, David Holl, who emphasizes that he considers himself accountable to the ideals of company founder, the late Mary Kay Ash. I had asked David for an interview during which we could talk about philosophy—specifically how Mary Kay's philosophy translates into the company's strategy. I was not disappointed.

I suspect that if you were to ask some of the now-unemployed people of recently failed companies about the reasons behind their firms' demise, they might list those same words: a lack of integrity, intelligence, and energy. They might also agree on how important it is to maximize today, think and act out of the box, and stay ahead of the curve. Further, if I were to list my own three rules of good corporate strategy, these same words would appear. Without integrity, intelligence, and energy, there is no support for the execution of good strategy.

"It all starts at the top," says Holl. While he believes that a company can find success without a charismatic CEO, Holl concedes that it certainly helps to have a charismatic leader like a Sam Walton or a Mary Kay Ash to lay the foundation. When speaking with Holl, it becomes very clear that he expects his senior leadership team to establish and uphold the level of integrity, intelligence, and energy that shaped Mary Kay's founding philosophies.

It has been my own experience as a business strategist that, unless the senior executive proactively supports iconoclastic behavior and thinking (think and act out of the box, stay ahead of the curve), those ideals simply cannot occur. In fact, without the proactive involvement of the senior leadership in fostering such behavior, the culture will revert to a staid, inflexible bureaucracy.

When I listened to David Holl, his personal accountability for leading those behaviors was evident—both to the legacy of Mary Kay and to the entire organization. "Mary Kay herself lived that way," he says. "Rather than just running the company centered around those principles, it's what she lived every day. Her ideals were ingrained in her character, and she made sure we understood that the firm's leadership had to live those ideals. Otherwise, she believed we would be much less likely to succeed."

Holl understands that companies can't just talk a good line; they have to earn the loyalty of their employees. As a corporate employer, Mary Kay Inc. is known for its careful selection of personnel. "Don't get me wrong," he observes. "We still make mistakes. But we try to be quick to react and correct them when we do." As a rule, Mary Kay studiously avoids large layoffs or downsizing. Holl says this has been possible because, "We stay as lean as possible and avoid spending ahead of our growth."

Within the company's one million-plus independent sales force, Mary Kay Inc. also seeks the goodwill that the founder engendered from the beginning in the consistency of her programs and practices. There are still grand and glorious prizes, generous commissions, and a teaching emphasis on developing leaders and instilling the Mary Kay values. "It is up to us to keep this opportunity as great as Mary Kay always wanted it to be," Holl observes.

> "We compete for our employees' hearts."

One of the ideals that Mary Kay always subscribed to—and today's management team wholeheartedly endorses—is that employees treat their customers in much the same way they are treated by the company. It is important to note that Mary Kay views its independent sales force as its primary customers. That is why they place so much importance on valuing and recognizing them.

Building trust and loyalty with its independent sales force is very important at Mary Kay Inc.

"We also compete for our employee's hearts," says Holl. "One of the most important things about leading is how you treat people. We learned from Mary Kay's example. We strive to treat our employees so well that they won't even think about leaving us to work somewhere else. And we are keenly aware that good people will always have other options."

That may be one reason why the corporate staff enjoys low turnover and remains so committed and empowered to solve customer–independent sales force–issues. "A very high percentage of inquiries are solved by the first contact with the company," says Holl, who adds that independent sales force customer service systems are designed to do just that. The balance of excellence and caring seems to drive every member of the team at every employee level to strive to provide the best service for every person with whom they come in contact.

Smart Risk Is a Necessity

The Mary Kay organization has always demonstrated a commitment to taking calculated risk. The founder herself demonstrated that commitment when she invested her life savings of $5,000 to launch the company, which opened just a month after she had lost her husband to a heart attack. Although thriving on creativity and risk, today's company leaders are also cautious about making sure to avoid the mistakes often associated with those same entrepreneurial attributes.

That competitive reality was clearly demonstrated by the company's technology philosophy upon entering the e-business arena. Though early to embrace the possibilities, Mary Kay Inc. was not the first to jump on the e-business bandwagon. "Of course, we saw the potential, but we also knew the exceptionally high risks. We knew we had to get it right and get it that way right out of the box," observes Holl, who thinks that spending time up front made a positive difference.

One of the corporate philosophies that the Mary Kay organization lives by is a "seek the best for others" approach, which is focused on its worldwide independent sales force as well as on its customer base. In the mid-1990s, Mary Kay executives clearly saw that the Internet held a great deal of potential for the company. For a company that thrives on staying on the leading edge of change, getting it right the first time around was their major concern.

The organization grappled with issues like what group was going to lead the online charge and how to handle the high traffic that would come to a Mary Kay Web site with its success throughout the independent sales force. One other issue was particularly relevant to Mary Kay Inc. as a direct selling company. The firm had always gone out of its way to make sure that the independent sales force was secure when it came to their customer relationships. "Simply put, we had to make sure that our independent sales force knew and trusted that our strategy was never to go around them to get to their customer. At the same time, we knew we needed their acceptance; we also needed that acceptance right away and in large numbers," said Holl, who can look back after seven years and be proud that Mary Kay's strategy was not only an instant and overwhelming success, but it was true to its commitment never to cut out its independent sales force. Holl and his leadership team were keenly aware that such behavior would have been a violation of Mary Kay Inc.'s bedrock principles and certainly no way to follow the "dance with who brung you" philosophy that prevails with regard to its relationship with the independent sales force.

Mary Kay's cautious creativity toward tailoring its Internet strategy has paid off.

By early 2004, some 90 percent of product orders from the independent sales force came via the Internet. Approximately 80,000 orders are processed any given week. Considered among the e-commerce giants, the company has continued to write programs that have proven of great value to its independent sales force, a huge percentage of whom also take advantage of Mary Kay's state-of-the-art educational and motivational online programs that have continually evolved since 1997.

The company's independent sales organization can now obtain all of their sales data online—this activity once involved massive printed reports that arrived after month-end. The company's technology strategy has been centered on convenience for its end-use customers and sales force. This has not only paid massive dividends in reduced costs and heightened customer service, it has also helped hundreds of thousands of individual business owners streamline the way they manage their own business systems and thus provide good service to their customers. All these innovations, plus the enhanced ability for a cosmetics empire to disseminate the latest beauty trends in a timely manner, may be why the firm has quietly become one of the largest e-businesses in the world in such a short time.

A Culture-Supported Strategy

When you mention "walk the talk" to an executive like David Holl, you get some idea of how the company defines excellence. Mary Kay founded the company on the Golden Rule: Do unto others as you would have them do unto you. Mary Kay believed that actions, not words, were the key to living out that principle. As with so many of her teachings, it became the standard for how the company operates. She believed that principle applied equally to the people who work for the company and those who comprise the independent sales force.

Culture might be defined as the internal environment of the company. It's often referred to as the unwritten rules by which the company does business. At Mary Kay Inc., the rules are clear. If it's difficult for you to work by these rules, you may not be a good fit for the company. The Mary Kay way instructs that leading is the opposite of controlling or demanding. A high premium is put on managers who can achieve goals at the same time as they inspire and lead. The model that developed first from Mary Kay's own brand of leadership has been refined over the years, and other companies continue to look to it even today—two decades after Mary Kay's philosophy was spelled out in her book, *Mary Kay On People Management*. It would be highly unlikely that a manager who is willing to sacrifice the well being of employees for the sake of personal gain would survive long in this culture. That ethos goes all the way to the top of the firm.

The company culture can be seen particularly in discussions about relationships among top executives. They are a diverse team with vastly different backgrounds, but Holl defines them more as a close-knit family than as business associates. There is little tolerance for those who only want to defend their territory. The focus is much more on how senior managers can work together to accomplish the firm's objectives. As Holl put it, "We truly care about one another."

When we look at the realities of today's competitive environment, it is my opinion that success depends upon speed, appropriate risk-taking, and trust. That explains why companies like Mary Kay do so well in challenging business environments as well as in good ones. Every manager and every employee has the freedom and the support that encourage them to strive for excellence. Rather than battling egos, maintaining the status quo mentalities, and cultural norms, the joint commitment to excellence among all members of the team allows the firm to avoid many of the bureaucratic and political traps that burden other organizations.

David Holl recognizes the critical role that the firm's culture plays in its ability tso sustain long-term profitability. "I think it's fair to say that a key focus of our job as members of the senior executive team—in addition, of course, to growing the company—is to sustain the Mary Kay culture," he says.

One of the ways that the culture plays out in Mary Kay Inc.'s corporate strategy is the continual high level of innovation within the firm.

The remarkable track record that the company has achieved for more than 40 years in the hotly competitive beauty industry speaks for itself. Mary Kay brands enjoy great customer loyalty. But there is more. Based on the most recent industry sales data and actual Mary Kay sales, in the United States, Mary Kay has ranked as the best-selling brand in the combined categories of facial skin care and color cosmetics for most of the last decade.

Part of the reason for that success has been the company's ability to tap into emerging markets like the elusive Gen-Xers and Gen-Yers, as well as the widely divergent international arena, while maintaining its loyal following among Baby Boomers and cultivating the youngest Echo Boomers.

Realizing that the company's domestic U.S. market was approaching the mature status (even though this market continues to show consistent growth), the company's leadership realized that it had to reinvent itself in the international arena to sustain its historical growth rates. The result has been success in a number of exploding international markets, including Mexico, Russia, and China. For a company like Mary Kay Inc., that also means that teams like technology and marketing and even research scientists have to think globally. Unlike many firms that keep their researchers in laboratories, Mary Kay's scientists travel the globe to understand the unique needs of each of its markets. "We listen to our customers," says David Holl. "That means that the people who create our products must have an intimate understanding of the independent sales force 'customers' as well as the end-use customers. You don't get that by living full-time in the lab; you've got to go to the source, and that's what our team does."

Transformational Management

David Holl likes to stress the tension between maintaining the firm's core culture and principles, while at the same time competing in a world that is different every day. The firm's competitors are some of the most respected companies in the world. They are known for their marketing and innovation savvy. In addition to that, Mary Kay—which advertises minimally—thrives in an industry where ad budgets are typically extremely large.

Admittedly, the company dances to the beat of a different drummer, preferring to spend what others might spend on ad dollars on the commissions, prizes, and recognition that are hallmarks of the firm. "As Mary Kay said, sometimes we fail forward to success," says Holl. "Yes, we face strong and smart competitors who continually create competitive challenges for us. It's the combination of our stable culture and our wonderfully creative entrepreneurial spirit that allows us to effectively compete." The combination apparently works, because the company has continued to excel even through some tough times.

On Thanksgiving Day 2001, company founder Mary Kay Ash passed away. The firm's leadership had been actively working on a transformational plan at the insistence of Mary Kay, who assumed the chairman emeritus title in 1987. However, when she had a stroke in 1996, the need for such action became even more evident. In many ways, the Founder herself put the plan in place.

It has been said that, "Sales is the heart of a company." What Mary Kay and a number of the firm's senior executives realized was that the leadership in the company's independent sales organization held the key to this firm's heart. With that in mind, Mary Kay Ash began working as far back as 1971 to pass her mantle of caring leadership to those who've reached the pinnacle of success in the independent sales force—more than 325 independent national sales directors worldwide. Mary Kay told them, "This company carries my name, but it has a life of its own." It became their role to sustain the principles and the culture of the founder. "That made a lot of sense," says Holl. "The independent national sales directors have embraced the challenge and executed it with brilliance."

In spite of the loss of its founder in 2001, the company has achieved record-breaking results in the three years since her passing. The worldwide independent sales force has grown from 800,000 to nearly 1.3 million. It's almost as if they were offering a personal salute to their departed leader, while contradicting skeptics who wondered what might happen to the company once its founder was gone.

In 2001, when I inquired about writing the leadership story of this company, I knew that it was an exceptional organization. What I saw was great strategy, a highly adaptive organization, and a corporate character founded on extremely high ethical standards. It should be no surprise that, when I assessed the company using my Corporate IQ measurement; the score was among the highest of any company that I had ever measured. That is a tribute not only to the firm's founder, Mary Kay Ash, but to the leadership team that has the wisdom and insight to lead the company forward into the 21st century.

Another one of those smart companies is Fidelity Investments. While the firm is well known for their mutual fund products, very little is known about how the firm is run. My investigation revealed that Fidelity is a leading edge company and warranted my attention.

FIDELITY INVESTMENTS: ONE OF THE TEN SMARTEST COMPANIES IN AMERICA

When you think about managers who communicate significance, I always think about Fidelity Investments. About four years ago a friend of mine was hired by Fidelity. It wasn't long before I got a phone call from him. He absolutely could not believe how the company treated its employees.

It seems that my friend was involved in one of those projects that requires working all night to get the job done. He had only been with the company for one day, when that need arose. Working through the night is not a normal expectation at Fidelity, unless you end up working in the information technology area where my friend worked. In that case, you often have to work on systems when they are not being used. That means the occasional evening or weekend.

In this particular case, the team was responding to an emergency that required the relocation of employees to a contingency site because of a broken water main. The team had to get everything in place by market opening the next day. In true Fidelity tradition, they worked long hours to ensure that employees reporting to the contingency site in the morning would have all the computer services they needed. They got the job done because they pulled together and set high standards for their own performance.

The following morning, my friend and his associates were called into a meeting with a company vice president. Executives at Fidelity's home office on the East Coast had heard about their exceptional commitment to complete their project the preceding evening and had instructed the local vice president to pass on their congratulations and a spot award check. Of course, a lot of praise went along with the money. When my friend called me and told me the story, all he could say is, "I've never been treated this well in my life." A few months later, the team was recognized a second time when the division president, along with a team of senior executives, flew to Dallas and presented each person with an outstanding service award plus another check, lunch at the Cattleman's Club, an inscribed crystal desk clock, and a framed picture of the team.

That is why Fidelity is one of the smartest companies in America. Everything they do focuses on the value that they place on their employees and their customers.

Strategy, Organization, and Character at Fidelity

Obviously, companies that score extremely high on the Corporate IQ assessment will have extremely good scores in the three major areas of strategy, organization, and character. Fidelity does so well for a number of reasons.

When it comes to strategy, a few areas are obvious. Fidelity Investments is fairly aggressive in the areas of advertising and promotion, key components of the assessment. There is another area in which the company's aggressiveness is not quite so obvious, the area of innovation.

One of the behind the scenes activities that characterizes Fidelity is a team that works on technology. The team is continually looking at new and emerging technologies that can impact the way Fidelity serves its clients. Imagine that you have the ability to receive constant updates on the status of your investment accounts on a device similar to a PDA. Add to that the ability to receive information no matter where you are in the world.

The emergence of the Internet as a global communications highway, plus the new technologies that will allow global access to the World Wide Web and personal e-mail, will change the way that we communicate. At Fidelity, a creative team is responsible for applying those technologies and constantly seeking new innovations that will enhance the firm's services.

Another important area of Fidelity is technology philosophy. Fidelity's national technology system is a marvel. With a number of somewhat identical technology centers around the country, Fidelity spends a great deal of money and time to ensure that multiple levels of redundancy exist.

Let us assume for a moment that a Fidelity customer is online, working on their account, and a massive power failure occurs in the region where the computing center is located. Due to the way that Fidelity's system is designed, the system will automatically move the client's connection to another regional computing center, and the client will never know what happened.

Fidelity Investments takes the same aggressive approach when it comes to corporate character. As I have already pointed out, they focus on the value of subordinates. Likewise, ethical standards are a focus in every aspect of the firm's business, and there is no tolerance for those who would violate Fidelity's standards. When it comes to quality and processes, a high level of openness exists around any opportunity to change processes that impact the customer.

Aggressive strategy, an adaptive organization, and unquestionable character—those are the prerequisites for success in a highly competitive uncertain environment. In the case of Fidelity, as with the other smart companies, a lot of attention is paid to these areas. Rather than resting on past successes, these smart companies are continually engaged in creating the future.

THE ULTIMATE MOTIVATOR

I started this chapter with a discussion of the significance principle. The most powerful aspect of the human personality is the desire to be recognized, appreciated, and valued. In the case of the two companies featured in this chapter, Mary Kay Inc. and Fidelity Investments, both are committed to making the significance principle a key aspect of their business. The success of these companies will hopefully provide valuable lessons for others that desire to be equally successful.

10

RAVE!

Inspired Excellence

A lot of people wonder how some of the great companies operate. The management literature talks a lot about "transformational leadership" and charismatic leaders, but limited information is available about how to create a great company. Without exception, the great companies operate on a principle that I call inspired excellence.

I believe that the acronym RAVE, Recognize-Appreciate-Value-Excellence, is a great way to understand how transformational leaders, and smart companies, lead their people. The idea of RAVE is simple. Recognize, appreciate, and value your people in everything you do. Add to that the standard of excellence in everything that the organization does, and you have a highly motivated organization. I'll briefly explain each of the four ideas.

First, *recognize* is what you do in public. It is one thing to tell someone that they did a great job on something. It's another entirely to call all their peers together and tell them what a great job someone did. Recognition as a public ceremony is the ultimate application of the significance principle. It conveys the idea of significance to the individual but, further, provides a ceremony in which to communicate it.

Appreciate deals with what might be called the little things that people do. It might simply be thanks for a project or a job well done. Appreciation is transactional in nature. That is, it occurs as a matter of course in conversations between a leader and one of their people. Appreciation is personal and reinforces the validity of what a leader does by recognizing others in a public setting.

Value has to do with the very foundation that underlies any relationship between people. It deals with the communication of just how important and capable a leader considers another person. I recently watched a new manager struggle in his job. As he began making decisions, he soon managed to make just about everyone mad. The problem is, the new manager had no idea what was going on.

The young manager was violating what I call the first rule of leadership.

T h e F i r s t R u l e o f L e a d e r s h i p

Before making any decision, get the counsel of those who will be affected by the decision, those who are passionate about the issue, and those who will have to carry out the decision.

The first rule of leadership addresses the issue of significance. If people feel discounted, you have just hit them right in the center of their being. As I have mentioned a number of times before, our need for significance is at the root of almost everything we think and do. The ability to communicate the fact that you truly value someone is one of the most important leadership skills that exist.

Excellence is the final factor that must be considered. Smart managers understand that excellence is the foundation of everything that a top organization does. Excellence has little to do with best practices or other comparison approaches. Excellence has to do with continually striving for the very best without regard to whether or not something has ever been done, or whether or not a competitor does it. Excellence also means that leaders must practice that principle in all their dealings with subordinates. Power trips, discounting, or control behaviors are not allowed in companies in which excellence is the standard. That means that managers who lack personal humility have no place in a company that practices RAVE.

One of the ten smartest companies in America is Southwest Airlines. Although branded by some as being a little corny, they proudly say that one of their most important corporate values is "love." Whether love is corny or not, hundreds of thousands of people apply to join this company every year. You have probably heard the song that goes, "looking for love in all the those goals. In some ways, that approach leans toward the Theory X view of Douglas McGregor. The opposite view, Theory Y, focuses on empowerment and involves little if any control.

As I pointed out earlier, some well-known companies have taken a Theory X approach to managing their people, and they have been able to sustain long-term profitability. I also mentioned that most of those companies were not dependent upon their peoples' ability to reinvent the firm continually. Those companies generally have products or product families with demand cycles of 50 to 100 years. I'm suggesting that few companies have the benefit of being in an industry segment in which their products are not continually changing. I agree that Theory X management will work for those companies. Even then, they will not maximize their profitability.

My research reveals that long-term success in a dynamic environment is clearly linked to management's ability to involve the firm's people in the creative process. What I have found in the smartest companies is what I like to call "inspired excellence." That is how Agilent operates as well.

Open Doors—Open Attitudes

I have previously discussed how the actions of a firm's leaders give meaning to the business philosophy of the firm. Ned Barnholt's commitment to spend a lot of informal time listening to associates as well as taking action on their ideas gives meaning to Agilent Technologies's entire business approach. The offices at a company provide the same kind of meaning.

Agilent has an open-door policy that is different from that of many other companies: a lot of the offices at Agilent have no doors. The absence of doors communicates openness and accessibility. Researchers will typically leave their projects out for all to see. Everyone who wanders by is encouraged not only to look at the project but to write the researcher notes that include ideas about the project. This "open doors—open attitude" policy creates an entire culture of innovation. The result is a string of new products on a continual basis. Isn't it interesting what happens when an entire organization is more concerned about team accomplishment rather than personal recognition? I suspect there is a lesson for aspiring senior executives in here somewhere.

To sustain the high level of innovation at Agilent, a system of account-ability is utilized. It involves four areas.

1. Goals
2. Metrics
3. Expectations
4. Empowerment

There is also a consistent focus on maintaining the unique culture of the company. First, they relish the idea of diversity. For starters, they hire and promote the brightest and best people. The result in that case is a diverse culture. They also promote diverse thinking. Pride of ownership is not really allowed. Everyone is encouraged to contribute their view on products, processes, or research. The result is an iconoclastic, out-of-the-box way of thinking and behaving that permeates everything the company does.

That interconnectedness carries over to the entire research and development structure of the firm. It would probably be an understatement to suggest that the firm's R&D is highly matrixed. There are four distinct research labs at Agilent: measurement research, molecular technology, photonics and electronics research, and precision instrumentation. In every case, proactive approaches link the three labs. I need to make an important point here. A lot of companies foster a competitive environment within the organization. At those companies, the last thing one lab would do is share a discovery with another lab. Some call that "siloing." The lack of interconnectivity or matrix links creates serious barriers to the exchange of internal information.

Earlier, I had talked about how everyone at Agilent is encouraged to be innovative. In addition to the three major labs, each business sector has product-specific labs to enable the firm further to stay at the leading edge of creating customer solutions. The creation of a high-trust, innovative culture plus the multiple-matrix structure results in extremely high levels of innovation. The result is a lot of profit potential in the form of new products. This is not a one-time event; it is a continual process of innovation.

An Ethics Anomaly

The past five years in corporate America have not been stellar when it comes to ethics. However, some companies stand out because of their exceptionally strong ethical standards. Agilent is one. As we have seen with some

When that occurs, that spark of excellence is passed on to another, then another. Ultimately, that spark of excellence finds its way into the life of a very important person: a customer. That spark of excellence creates a company that becomes a consistent first choice in the hearts of those who deal with it.

It is this simple: inspired excellence is a choice. It is hard work, but for those exceptionally smart companies, it is not an option. It is the only way they want to do business. It's spelled RAVE.

11

CREATING THE ULTIMATE CUSTOMER EXPERIENCE

Ted Brown is one of those unmistakable people called a "native Texan." He looks the part. His usual uniform is jeans, boots, a checkered shirt, and one of those gigantic belt buckles that looks like it weighs at least 15 pounds. Ted is also known for his unusual sense of humor and his willingness to engage just about anyone who walks in the door with his unique form of personal harassment. Of course, Ted drives a pickup truck and is an avid outdoorsman, but that's not the end of the story.

Ted grew up in the car repair business. A number of years ago, he decided that the industry needed someone they could go to who would seek the best for them. Ted started his own business, and his reputation for honesty and expertise soon spread. Ted did so well that he was able to build his own repair facility, complete with a customer waiting area well furnished with couches and recliners, all facing a wood-burning fireplace. It would not be exaggerating to say that Ted created a real first-class facility.

Over the years, the faces don't change much at Brown's Automotive. Every few years, there is a retirement, but aside from that, there is no such thing as a revolving door when it comes to the staff at the firm. One of the things Ted just won't tolerate is dishonesty. If someone comes in with a loose battery cable, he won't accept a mechanic or service writer who tries to turn that into a $300 repair bill. In fact, if it's a loose battery cable, Ted and his people fix the problem and won't consider charging for it.

The other thing one quickly discovers about Ted's organization has to do with their knowledge. In this day of technological change, one may go to a nondealer repair facility and be told that they do not have either the equipment or the knowledge to correct the technical problem your automobile has. That just doesn't happen at Brown's.

Ted Brown has created what I call the "ultimate customer experience" for those who are fortunate enough to take their car to him. It's all about what's best for the customer. Underneath all that Texas bravado is a man committed to integrity. More than that, he runs his business exactly as if it was where he would take his own car.

A visit to the waiting room in Brown's Automotive tells the story another way. "I drove in from Sherman," one man said to me. Sherman, it turns out, is well over an hour's drive from Ted's shop. In one case, a customer had a transmission problem over 200 miles away. Rather than trust anyone other than Ted Brown to fix it, the customer had her car towed 200 miles to Ted's shop.

That is what happens when a company establishes the ultimate customer experience for those it serves. Of course, every company has its financial and service limits, but the smart companies will consistently challenge those limits. Their leaders understand that when a company provides customers with an experience of that nature, they become customers for life.

A lot has been written about the "voice of the customer" and about understanding customer needs. In the case of smart companies, they generally take a proactive approach to customers. Rather than simply responding to customer pressures or conducting the obligatory customer survey, smart companies proactively search for new ways to create the ultimate customer experience. They understand that service and customer relationships change and, in many cases, the customer is not aware of their needs. Smart companies understand how to stay ahead of the curve in considering customer needs. As technologies change, they try to anticipate the new customer challenges those developments will create. Kingston Technology anticipates extremely well. I was fortunate to have the opportunity to spend a day at Kingston's home office in California and visit with a number of their people, including the founders of the company.

KINGSTON TECHNOLOGY: ONE OF THE TEN SMARTEST COMPANIES IN AMERICA

Kingston Technology was founded in 1987 by John Tu and David Sun. Over the past 16 years, Kingston has grown from humble beginnings to become a global leader in the computer memory area. They have also become a leader in logistics. Their customer list includes global technology giants as well as smaller firms.

They are especially well known for their exceptional commitment to employees, vendors, and customers. They have a reputation of being a wonderful place to work, and their vendors hold them in the highest esteem. As a result of their employee and vendor relationships, their customer loyalty is among the highest in the United States. So strong is their commitment to their customers, Kingston has been known to pay for a customer to ship their computer to them (and back), even though the customer has purchased only a $30 piece of Kingston memory. Not surprisingly, in most cases, the problem is not with the Kingston product. Even then, the company is pleased to return the customer's repaired computer for no charge. I am sure you will agree, Kingston Technology is a unique company.

Corporate Humility

You don't hear a lot of people talk today about corporate humility. A lot of people think that humility has to do with the way you act, but it really has to do with the way you think. That is important, because how you think ultimately determines how you act. Humility is a way of life for some people as well as for some companies. Kingston Technology is one of those companies.

One of the things that smart leaders focus on is what I call "meaning." Smart leaders use action to give meaning to the practices and principles by which they want their organization to run. As you enter Building A at the Kingston Technology headquarters in Fountain Valley, California, it looks a lot like any other successful company. When you get to the second floor of the building, however, your impression will change quickly. Except for a few people who have a job-related need for an office, there aren't many offices. There are no partitions. In fact, as you look out over any large room in the building, all you see is desks and people.

Around one corner, sitting out in the middle of the room, is a desk with a nameplate reading "David Sun." A hundred feet or so away is another desk with a nametag reading "John Tu." On every side of those desks are more

FIGURE 11.1 *A Philosophy of Leadership*

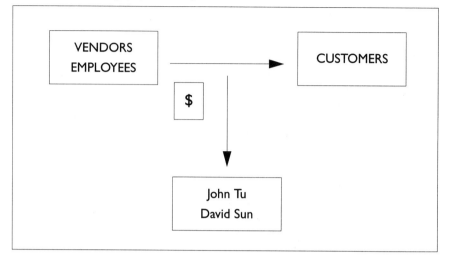

desks. The people at those desks do myriad jobs. Some are new hires who are just learning the ropes. Others are seasoned veterans working with major customers. What makes this setup unique is that David Sun and John Tu are the founders and senior executives of this almost $2 billion company. John and David conduct their business in an open setting alongside their people. "That is one of the most important ways we communicate with our people," said David Sun. "We, as the founders and senior executives, are totally dependent on our people. They make the profit, not us. We can't execute—they can!"

David went on to explain how he and John work together to coach and inspire their team toward excellence. John, the eldest of the two, is the exact opposite of David. While David is always moving and extroverted, John tends to think about something for a long time before he says anything. They confess that the first few years of their relationship were a bit challenging at times, but they eventually realized that they are a powerful combination.

After talking about the company for a while, David asked if he could draw a picture on the board. He wanted to give me a clear picture of their philosophy of leadership. (See Figure 11.1.)

As he spoke, David became very animated. Basically, he views the diagram as the secret to their business. "I am a simple man," said David. "John and I believe that if we take care of and reward the people who make the profits, and we also take extremely good care of our vendors, that the outcome will be exceptional care for our customers. If we do that (and he pointed at the downward arrow with the dollar sign next to it), we will make more money. We always make sure that we share our financial success with our people. After all, they are the ones that make the profit."

John and David believe that the location of their offices gives meaning to their philosophy of business. They are open about everything. They conduct their business in the open for all to hear. It is a way of establishing high levels of trust within the organization. They also believe that it really helps them understand how the company is working, because they can listen to their team as they deal with various issues.

A Run on the Bank

A little after noon on a sunny California afternoon, the staff at a local Wells Fargo branch in Fountain Valley became suspicious. In a little over 30 minutes, the lobby of the bank had filled up. It became so crowded that there was almost no more room for anyone to get into the building. It was not a robbery; it was people putting money in the bank.

It seems that on that particular day in 1996, John Tu and David Sun had sold an 80 percent stake in their company for $1.5 billion. As each employee returned from lunch that day, they found an envelope and a check on their desk. There was also a personal thank-you note from David and John. In some cases, the checks were well over $100,000. It was David and John's way of sharing the profit that the team had produced.

When all of the Kingston people got their checks, many headed for the local Wells Fargo branch located nearby. That is why the lobby filled up. All those Kingston people wanted to deposit their checks. At one point, a Wells Fargo employee stood up and yelled, "Congratulations, Kingston people!" The crowd, still waiting in line to make their deposits, roared and applauded.

When it comes to corporate humility, David Sun and John Tu went to great lengths to make sure that the story of the bonuses stayed inside the Kingston family. Much to their dismay, the story was picked up by the national media and made most of the prime-time news broadcasts. Even today, they are hesitant to talk about the story, preferring instead to focus on the wonderful accomplishments of their people.

You Are Empowered to Be Excellent

From a formal standpoint, Kingston has a program that is designed to foster high levels of innovation. It is simply called a continuous program improvement, and it is administered through the company's Lotus Notes program on their network. People are encouraged to submit ideas, and every idea is carefully considered by a Kingston team. But it is not quite that simple.

David Sun refers to himself as a jumpy individual. He says that he is always concerned that a competitor will get to a new customer idea first. David has a lot of ideas. He likes to go and test his ideas on different people in the firm. If he gets buy-in, he encourages the employee to go forward and try the idea. If he doesn't get buy-in, he may try a couple more times. If he still does not have success, he may ask if the employee will go ahead and try the idea just to see if it works. If the idea works, David recognizes the employee. "If it doesn't work, I make sure to go to the employee and say 'Boy was I stupid,'" says David with a smile.

Kingston, like other smart companies, does not punish people for mistakes. In fact, they recognize people who step out and take risks, even if sometimes they fail. From top to bottom, the firm's leadership realizes that the creativity needed to stay at the forefront of their industry necessarily involves some failures.

Trust drives innovation in the company. In one case, Richard Kanadjian, technology manager, concluded that the company needed to invest in some expensive test equipment to stay ahead in a new product area. Richard went to visit with John Tu and explained that he needed to spend $1.5 million on the equipment. David immediately told him to make the investment. Richard recalled the meeting in our conversation. "I was a bit shocked at how quickly he backed me. I decided to go ahead and tell him that I really needed two sets of testing equipment if I was to be able to do the best job for our customers. He didn't even blink when I told him it would be over $3 million for all of the equipment." Richard went on to explain how much it meant to him for someone to put such trust in him.

Another team member, Mark Leathem, told a similar story. It seems that he had figured out that they were paying $15 per hit for advertising their product on a major Internet search engine site. After some investigation, he realized that the product they were advertising only cost about $15. "I thought that it would be a lot more powerful if we gave away the product than just paying for someone to visit our site," he said. "I decided to strike a deal with one of our technology partners to offer free product through their Web site. That was great for them, and we got to put our products into the hands of some brand new customers."

After a while, he realized that he had not told anyone about what he was doing. He decided to visit with David and explain what he had done. David's response: "What a great idea. We're going to sell a lot more products by getting a few samples into the hands of customers than we ever could by paying someone for hits on their Web site."

While at the company, I ran into a new hire who had only been at the firm for a little over six months. It seems that his desk was next to David Sun's. He confessed that he was a little overcome with the way that Kingston did business. At first, he really could not believe it. One day, he had occasion to visit with David Sun in the hallway. During the conversation, he mentioned how much he appreciated how the people at Kingston, including himself, were treated. Much to his surprise, David explained to him that he is one of the people at the company who can "execute." David went on to explain that he and John cannot execute. He explained that the people make things happen, and they want employees to understand that they are the ones who are really important because, "They make the profit, not the founders." It had taken six months, but Bill Kuo finally understood that it all was for real. He really was valued and appreciated. That knowledge had an enormous impact on him.

Strategy at Kingston

During my visit with the founders, John made a point of talking about the firm's strategy. Unlike a lot of companies, Kingston does not have a five-year plan. They usually operate with strategies that focus on fairly short horizons. But that does not tell the entire story.

During my tour, I was shown a new testing facility for a product that is not yet available to the public. The company started working on testing the product, buying related equipment, and working with the new technology in 2003. Due to the high-trust relationship that exists between Kingston and some of its major vendors, the vendors are willing to provide prototypes of new products to Kingston long before the products are commercially available. Because of this ahead-of-the-curve approach, Kingston has a decided edge when the product finally comes on line.

Richard Kanadjian made an interesting comment when I was visiting with him. "I had to forget a lot of what I'd learned during my MBA coursework when I came to Kingston." He went on to explain that Kingston never tries to utilize all of its production capacity. In fact, when they reach 50 percent capacity, they usually begin to think about expanding their manufacturing capacity. "We know that our customers depend on us if they get into a bind. If a customer calls and says they need 10,000 units in a week, we make it happen. We have the capacity, and all of our team is more than willing to go the extra mile to make sure we meet the customer's needs."

In one case, an assembly line employee advanced an idea regarding a riveting process. The employee believed that it could be done in a much shorter period of time. As a result of a lot of empowerment and some creative thinking on the part of the employee, the process was shortened from six to eight weeks to one week.

Kanadjian also said that Kingston breaks down processes to a bare minimum. He talked about how the finance department does not get involved in approving expenditures. As most people know, getting finance's approval can be a real bottleneck when it comes to meeting customer needs. David Sun mentioned that during our visit. "The finance department is there to keep records of our successes. We make customer decisions really quickly, so we can't afford to run decisions through some bureaucratic process. We are all about speed of execution."

Another unique aspect of Kingston is its quality program. Unlike some companies, Kingston does not use statistical process control to test product quality. Kingston has designed robotic testing equipment that enables them to test 100 percent of their products before shipping. "We believe that our customers have the right to expect the very best from us," said Kanadjian, "and that means that we do not ship any product until we have tested it and know that it works."

Another strategy of Kingston is its approach to cycle time. A lot of companies are willing to live with a one month cycle time. That is, they feel pretty good about themselves if they can ship an order within one month of when they receive it. At Kingston, they like to see just how fast they can turn an order. Frequently, a customer will call with a large order and need it within a week. Kingston consistently meets their deadline.

"In a lot of cases, we turn an order in 24 hours," said Kanadjian. "In fact, for many customers who place orders in the morning, we manufacture their products as well as deliver them before the end of the day." David Sun believes that those short cycle times are one of the key differentiators between Kingston and the competition. He believes that the flat structure of the organization, the can-do spirit of the team, and the empowered nature of the environment allow them to do things that their competitors just cannot do. During our visit, David Sun did confess one fear that he had that was related to his competitors. "If I see our competitors treating their employees like we treat ours, I'll be scared. Until then, I think we have an advantage because of our team. We are capable of doing things that other companies simply cannot do, and John and I owe it all to our people."

The Kingston People

One of the foundations of the company's approach is its hiring process. When asked about their philosophy in this area, David Sun said: "We hire good people; we want humble, modest people who get along well with others." David and John Tu went on to explain that they are willing to take a lot of risk on people as well. Once someone is on board, the entire team has the task of helping each person to maximize their potential. David and John also explained that the company's turnover is probably about one-fourth that of their competitors. They also credited their people with the company's ability to be so flexible and responsive. "We can move fast because our people are so experienced," said David. "Our advantage is that we can take a challenging task and assign it to a team that is 90 percent veterans and only 10 percent rookies. We know how to work together, cut out all the bull, and get the job done. That's our advantage."

Another one of those exceptionally smart companies is Luxottica Retail. You may know them best by the name LensCrafters, which is one of their subsidiaries. What you will discover is that, like the other smart companies, they understand how to create the ultimate customer experience. One of the ways they do that is to "create the ultimate associate experience." By focusing their efforts on their people and their customers, Luxottica Retail's brands continue to grow and to thrive.

LUXOTTICA RETAIL: ONE OF AMERICA'S TEN SMARTEST COMPANIES

Ask any tennis player what their most burning question about tennis might be, and you might be surprised. Around the clubhouse and in other tennis venues, you will often hear players compare the shots they make in the warm-up with the shots they make during a match.

The reason this is such a topic of interest is simply that most players would love to be able to make some of the shots they make in the warm-up during the match. On more than one occasion, I have seen people hit high-speed flat shots in their warm-up session, only to follow up with a high percentage of shots out of bounds during the match.

Experienced players will tell you that the explanation is simple. It's all about having the ability to relax. In a match, the average player will get tense when a difficult shot comes along. That same player, in a relaxed pregame session, is usually able to make some pretty impressive shots, all because they are relaxed.

In analyzing the smartest companies in America, I have found that they go to great lengths to make sure that their employees are relaxed. That does not mean that there is no incentive to be excellent. It does mean that employees feel that they are surrounded by people who care about them and the job that they do. It means that they work for a company that is extremely hesitant to terminate someone and will do everything possible to help that employee learn to be exceptional. There's a reason for that. You see, when people are relaxed, they can make some "incredible shots." That is also why the companies that made the "top ten smartest companies in America" list focus a lot of their efforts on *fun*. It seems that companies that excel not only work hard, but they play hard as well.

One such company is Luxottica Retail. Although it's listed on the New York Stock Exchange, chances are you are not too familiar with the company—not, that is, until you hear the names of their companies: LensCrafters, Sunglass Hut, Watch Station, and EyeMed Vision Care. In most cases, people are familiar with at least one if not all of those companies.

Strategy: A Culture of Excellence

At the heart of this somewhat young (a little over 20 years of existence) company is a focus on excellence in all three major areas: strategy, organization, and character. Again, when I use the word *excellence,* I am not referring simply to a company that tries to be the best; I am talking about a company that is committed to creating the exceptional. Keep in mind that, at smart companies like Luxottica Retail, excellence applies to all three areas of the firm: strategy, organization, and character.

As I previously noted, attributes like excellence create sustainability. Smart leaders understand that any erosion in the character of the firm leads to deteriorated profit and performance. At Luxottica Retail, the culture of excellence is the shared responsibility of the entire executive and leadership team.

One aspect of transformational leadership is the setting of somewhat outrageous goals. The aspirations of Luxottica Retail reveal a lot about how such an approach can create a firm that is continually striving to achieve

FIGURE 11.2 *Luxottica Retail's Mission and Vision*

Luxottica Retail's Mission: "To Serve and Inspire with Excellence"

Luxottica Retail's Vision: "To be the retailer of the Century"
- The Best Place to Work
- Best Place to Shop
- Best Place to Invest
- The Best at Helping the World See

higher levels of excellence. Take a look at Luxottica Retail's mission and vision in Figure 11.2.

One of the things that the organization has is the "world's best workplace committee." The work of the organization revolves around the firm's values and its desire to ensure that their values are carried out continually in practice. Here are those values.

- Uncompromising integrity
- Respect
- Teamwork
- Fun
- Trust
- Quality
- Innovation

Those values came out of LensCrafter's original value statement of doing "the right thing for the customer." Interestingly, those values are reflected in the company pins, called "vision pins," that are given to all 25,000 employees. Each pin comes in a package with the words *Mission-Vision-Values,* and the pin is a triangular shape with the words that summarize the firm's mission—*Serve, Inspire, and Excel*—around the border.

In visiting with Scott Stoelting (senior director of corporate culture), Carol Spicer (senior director of human resources), and Kathy Clark (director of communications), I discovered that the organization had added another value of "uncompromising integrity." This came about as the result of associate feedback. While integrity was implied under the value of trust, associates indicated that in the current business atmosphere of many corporate fiascos, they wanted the entire organization to stand proudly for uncompromising integrity. The decision was made to put uncompromising integrity at the top of the list. The team believed that every aspect of the organization, from how individuals were treated to how customers were handled, had used that value as a foundation. That attitude is not uncommon at the smartest companies.

Integrity, Trust, Turnover, and Satisfied Customers

One thing that separates smart companies from others is their rejection of a concept that I call "acceptable neglect." We all know that it's possible to intimidate an employee group into a few quarters' or, in some cases, a number of years' acceptable performance. At the same time, if you utilize such tactics, you should not expect to have high levels of trust within your organization. Yes, it is possible to achieve a minimal level of customer satisfaction with that approach, but that approach will never achieve exceptional customer relationships. At this point, I would expect the more insightful reader to understand why some of America's old-line companies did not make the "ten smartest companies in America" list.

As I have said a number of times before, it is possible to intimidate people to a point where they achieve acceptable customer service. Those same employees have little interest in achieving excellence. I recently saw a sign at a company I was visiting. It was posted on an employee's cubical wall.

Smart companies understand that you never achieve long-term success on the backs of your people. While some companies burn out their people, badgering and intimidating them while simultaneously sustaining profitability, they do not maximize profit.

Luxottica Retail and other exceptional smart companies understand the basic rule of maximum performance: excellence produces excellence! If you are committed to treating your people with excellence, they will treat your customers with excellence. It is not rocket science. If you want to create the ultimate customer experience, you must start the process by creating the ultimate employee experience. As I have visited with the Luxottica Retail team, that principle oozes out of every conversation. Not only do they pass it on to the customers, they pass it on to the world.

Luxottica Retail's approach pays off in the hiring area as well. While others in the retail business try to find ways to deal with turnover rates in the 50 percent to 100 percent area, LensCrafters full-time positions maintain an industry low of 19 percent rate. (Total Luxottica Retail turnover for all brands, full-time and part-time, is at 45 percent.) I guess people want to work where they are recognized, appreciated, and valued.

The Best at Helping the World to See!

Every year, a significant percentage of Luxottica Retail's 25,000 people apply to go on a "mission trip." Working in conjunction with Lions Club International to gather discarded prescription eyeglasses, the Luxottica Retail team sends groups of 25 to 30 member teams of doctors and volunteers worldwide to provide the gift of sight to others. This team provides free eye exams and recycled glasses to those who cannot afford them around the globe.

But it takes more than just the collection of eyeglasses to pull this off. Throughout the year, Luxottica Retail's people sponsor fund-raising events for their charitable arm, the LensCrafters Foundation. Rather than being a one-time event, a mission trip is the culmination of the efforts of the people of Luxottica Retail from around the United States and Canada. The program now conducts one international mission every month. Participating in such events is a way of life throughout the entire organization, from home office to stores.

The stories of the people they have helped are inspiring. In one case, an old woman had never been able to see her two baby granddaughters. In another, a young boy had never been able to see well enough to write at school. In story after story, we see that the efforts of the people of LensCrafters, Sunglass Hut, and Watch Station—the Luxottica Retail team—are experiencing the exhilaration of helping others in a unique way.

Sometimes . . . Things Go Wrong

I have been focusing on a lot of the great things about this company. In my investigation, I also asked questions about how the firm handles problems. I want to introduce a word that Luxottica Retail does not use but that really describes their approach in dealing with problems: *reconciliation.* The word conveys a difference between parties in which the resolution is two-sided, not just one-sided as we see in many organizations. In living out their value of uncompromising integrity, the firm's leadership has set up some unique approaches.

It all starts with a "we're slow to let someone go" attitude at the top, according to Carol Spicer, senior director of human resources. In listening to Spicer talk about their process, it became clear that the process is all about nurturing associates. At a lot of companies, the process is more about "building a case" so you do not get sued. "The first thing we do is look at ourselves as well as the employee," says Spicer. "We try to discover deficiencies in our training of the employee; we give them personal attention to make sure that they clearly understand the job we are asking them to do. Then we develop an action plan that includes training as well as goal setting." There are some offenses for which there is immediate termination.

Step two is initiated only after the employee has failed to correct deficiencies. That occurs in the form of a written warning. After every effort to save the employee has been made, the third and final step is termination. The company tries everything to make sure that the employee understands that the power to stay with the company rests solely in their own hands. "We focus on making our people successful," says Spicer. "When we get to that final step of termination, we like to believe that we have done everything possible to help the individual have a rewarding career. But it does take commitment from both sides, and regrettably in this world, that does not always happen."

Finding and Keeping the Best of the Best

Luxottica Retail, according to Carol Spicer, is extremely aggressive in its recruiting approach. The objective is not just to fill slots but to find and hire the very best. They utilize numerous sources to accomplish that objective. "We spend a lot of time networking," she says. The end result is one of the lowest turnover rates in the retail industry.

Another tool that the firm uses to keep its best is to recognize exceptional performance. During the year, the company features inspiring stories of associates in the VIP (Very Inspired People) newsletter. In addition, numerous award and recognition programs are designed to honor exceptional service in more than 13 different categories. Luxottica even has an award to honor vendors who go above and beyond to deliver great service called The Extra Mile Pin.

Luxottica Retail practices what I call "RAVE Leadership." That means that you *recognize, appreciate,* and *value* your people who are *excellent* and do excellent things. I consistently find these practices when looking at exceptional companies. After all, great companies are not about bricks and mortar—they're about the people who engage in greatness.

A Commitment to Innovative Excellence

"That's my personal mission," said Mildred Curtis, senior vice president of human resources, as she talked about Luxottica Retail's approach to people and excellence. "I believe that the foundation of everything I do must focus on making sure we are a culture of excellence. It all starts with our people, and getting and keeping great people is my job."

It does not take long to figure out that Mildred Curtis absolutely loves her job. "I knew from the moment I walked in the front door that this was a special company. I don't know how to say it, but you can feel the difference when you enter the premises of the company," said Curtis. A special bond clearly exists between the members of the Luxottica team. "We are a fun group," said Curtis. "We are all about excellence, but fun is at the top of the list as well." There are no examples to support "fun."

It is clear that an almost invisible force propels this group of people. "We focus on creating tenure," she continued. She went on to explain that the senior executives had studied their most productive people, and that the more tenured people clearly are the most productive. "The invisible difference," said Curtis, "is the power of doing things for others. I am convinced that, as our people go out into the community or go out of their way to help a customer, that it touches our peoples' hearts. Doing good things for others changes you."

I had heard that comment before as I visited with others at the company. Some used the word *different,* and others used the word *special,* but they were really saying the same thing. When people step out and go beyond themselves to help someone else, they create a pride in serving that changes everyone involved. Regardless of how it is conveyed, the invisible difference is what drives every individual in the company to focus on taking the personal responsibility to discover new opportunities for achieving excellence.

The result is a senior vice president of human resources who sees her job as different from the way most in similar positions at other firms view theirs. Mildred Curtis has a singular focus as being the "champion for the Luxottica Retail culture." "In everything I do," said Curtis, "I continually ask myself if our actions will ensure that we maintain a culture of excellence." As with the other smart companies, excellence begins with how the firm's people are treated. "Excellence also means that we stretch people beyond what they think they can do," said Curtis.

According to Mildred Curtis, the focus on excellence within the firm makes her job of external recruiting much easier. She explained that exceptional people are attracted to the company. "It's like there was a magnet here or something, we are continually amazed that really exceptional people find us and ask for the opportunity to join us."

Collaboration Drives Innovation

Mildred Curtis spent a lot of time talking about collaboration. She explained how it begins with the hiring process. Although the human resources team begins the process with an in-depth assessment, from that point forward, it's all collaboration. "There is an emphasis on gathering input and support for everyone that a new employee would work with, from the hiring manager to the entire team."

The idea of collaboration is prevalent in the area of corporate strategy as well. Iconoclastic behavior is not just talked about, it is expected. Managers are empowered to challenge executives. "Strategy is not just a top-down process," said Curtis. "The managers that are working with customers have a lot of insight. We encourage every member of our team to help us find better ways to serve our customers. There is no pride of ownership here; we really cherish the input of everyone on our team. We always keep our customers and our people at the top of the priority list. That means we value their input."

The Luxottica executive team goes to great lengths to reinforce what I will call "servant leadership." Servant leadership is founded on corporate humility. The Luxottica leadership team is proactive about communicating that idea. There is no tolerance for ego trips. Office doors are always open, and every executive welcomes a member of the company who wants to visit about a concern or an opportunity.

The executive team goes out of their way to send that message. They enjoy walking into the company lunchroom at their headquarters location and having lunch with a group of their people. It's all about the healthy exchange of ideas, never about top-down communication.

When asked about the foundation that underlies Luxottica's success, there is no hesitation. Curtis believes that the involvement in helping others through the Gift of Sight program has enormous impact on the entire organization. "Our people go out into their communities or to the far reaches of the world in order to provide vision for those who cannot afford it. When they return, they are changed because of what they did for someone else," says Curtis. "It establishes a foundation of care that touches everything we do as a company."

Curtis went on to talk about changes she saw in the company. She talked about how their focus on a culture of excellence was being blended with a culture of innovation. That message is supported by an expectation of empowerment, according to Curtis. "We are trying to build a company in which every member of the team sees himself or herself as a leader," she said. "Let's be honest. Only our people and not our senior executives have the ability to live the ideas of excellence and innovation in the lives of our customers."

A View from the Top

Kerry Bradley, chief operating officer for Luxottica Retail, is a 16-year veteran of the company. Prior to joining Luxottica Retail, he spent his early years in advertising and brand management with one of the top consumer brands companies in the world. He was approached by a team of former associates who asked him to join this new company called LensCrafters. What sold him on making the change was their desire to build an exceptional company with a big "heart."

"A lot of people think you cannot be a caring organization and also be a large company," said Bradley. "The team that acquired LensCrafters 20 years ago believed that it was possible to grow and become a large organization while at the same time having a lot of heart. It turns out they were right. When you give to others, you always get more in return than you gave."

When you get down to it, Luxottica Retail is not obsessed with profit. "We are obsessed with helping others," said Bradley. "We believe if you do your very best to help your customers, both paying and nonpaying [their charity work], plus have the same obsession about caring for your people, the profits are inevitable. It's just that simple."

The result, according to Kerry Bradley, is a Luxottica team that has an unbelievable passion for all that they do, including caring for the company's 12 million customers. As I listened to Kerry Bradley talk, I realized that the passion he was talking about was clearly not some gimmick to get people to perform well; it was a passion that he felt as well.

Speaking of profit, the company, along with the rest of the retailers in the United States and Canada, was hit pretty hard. "We were a bit disappointed with our performance," said Bradley. I was almost amused at the reason. Luxottica Retail did not have the disastrous year that some had in 2003. In fact, they achieved a really nice profit result. "Actually, we were hoping to achieve our growth goals as well as our profit goals," he said. "I know a lot of people would have liked to have made level profits in 2003, and we are thankful that our profits held. It's just that when you are part of a company that stretches, you feel like you've failed if you aren't able to hit those lofty goals."

In spite of their relative disappointment, the company continues to produce pretax profits (as a percentage of revenues) that are 100 to 400 percent higher than their competitors. It is clear that yesterday is not what consumes this company's leadership. In fact, they are so consumed with tomorrow that their latest initiative is all about creating the future.

For starters, the executive level leadership program, historically offered only to senior executives, was rolled out to the company's managers throughout the United States and Canada. "We realized that we needed a great leadership program at all levels if we wanted all our people to take charge of their future," said Kerry Bradley. They paired that initiative with another effort that targets creating an even more creative, innovative, and explosive organization. "There's nothing wrong with what we are today," he said. "At the same time, we believe we can be significantly better in the future. That's the charter for our entire organization. We want to create an even better future for our people, our customers, our stockholders, and those we serve around the world."

At the time of the interview with Kerry Bradley, Luxottica Group had entered into an agreement to acquire one of its largest competitors. This smart company clearly has little interest in resting on its laurels. They are intent on creating a company that will make sure that they fulfill one of their prime objectives: "To be the retailer of the century." It should surprise no one that they are already on track to fulfill that dream.

SMART COMPANIES AND THE
ULTIMATE CUSTOMER EXPERIENCE

While I was working on this chapter, I needed to shop at one of the oldest retail companies in America. I could not help but compare the extreme differences between that company and the smart companies I have studied. It should surprise no one that the smart retailers are growing and maximizing profit. That, of course, is what separates the smart companies from the not-so-smart companies. The smart companies understand that customers really are important and how you care for them goes straight to the bottom line.

12

STRATEGIC FOCUS

Finding Your Way in a Chaotic World

By now, you have figured out that a lot of the debate in the academic world has to do with how organizational leaders should think about chaos. On one side of the argument are the traditionalists, who suggest that there is no need to account for complexity and random events in the competitive environment. For the traditionalists, there is no need for a company to question the industry or products in which it competes.

This discussion would not be complete unless I mentioned the fad *du jour* crowd. In reality, a lot of companies' strategies are driven by the latest fad. In those cases, the employees of such companies must deal with another new fad every 12 to 24 months. Most of these fads can be effective tools only if the firm's leadership understands that a complex mental model is required if the firm is in a complex environment. That's another way of affirming Dr. Seuss's statement: "When you know where things are out of whack, then you know how to get them back in whack."

Another school of thinking revolves around complexity. One group takes a Darwinian approach, which assumes that organizations will self-organize. Another group focuses on the inability of the human mind to deal with complexity, suggesting that such "bounded rationality" prohibits the development of effective strategy for the future. They believe that all good strategies emerge after the fact.

Complex dynamic systems is the mental model that I propose in this book. The system has two general characteristics and both must be accounted for in the development of corporate strategy: complexity and speed of change. Fads don't do that, emergence does not do that, nor does either the complex adaptive or the traditional approach. Research reveals many possible levels of complexity as well as speed of environmental change which with firms must deal. Complex dynamic systems are simply reality.

STRATEGIC FOCUS

Leaders who create strategies, organization, and character that are appropriate for their company's competitive context can keep the company operating in the profit zone. To put that another way, if the competitive context is level 4 (rapidly changing, highly complex, moderately high levels of uncertainty), the smart leader will focus on creating aggressive strategies, a highly adaptive organization, and the highest level of corporate character. Smart companies not only deliver creative destruction into the lives of their competitors, they rapidly adapt to those same destructive efforts of their competitors. That is how a company can proactively anticipate as well as reactively adapt to stay in the profit zone.

COSTCO WHOLESALE CORPORATION: ONE OF THE TEN SMARTEST COMPANIES IN AMERICA

The November 24, 2003, edition of *Fortune* had an interesting article title: "The Only Company Wal-Mart Fears." The article is about the membership warehouse club, Costco. Consider some of the statistics cited in the article.

- Sam's Club has 71 percent more locations than Costco, yet as of August 31, 2003, Costco had 5 percent more sales.
- The average Costco warehouse generates almost double the revenue of a Sam's warehouse.[1]

"We take what some might think is a pretty radical approach," said Richard Galanti, chief financial officer of Costco Wholesale Corporation. "Corporate America has really developed a downsized, efficiency, and cost-cutting mindset, particularly when it comes to controlling labor and benefits expenses. Some companies control these expenses by figuring out how 'little' they must pay their employees and how much of the health care costs they can pass on to their employees. While we agree with the idea of cost efficiency, we believe the rest of that stuff is mostly about sacrificing the well-being of your employees in order to increase profits; we don't buy that. We believe you can do both."

I would agree: Costco's attitude does run contradictory to the general thinking at most companies. The same could be said for all of our top ten smartest companies. They have little interest in sacrificing the well being of their employees for the sake of profit. In fact, they all believe that profits will be increased if a company goes out of its way to treat every member of the team with the ultimate in respect and care, including compensation.

"Why in the world would a company not understand that having well-paid employees with great benefits, management that cares, and unquestionable ethics would not lead to higher profits?" said Galanti. "Our turnover is one-third that of the retail industry as a whole; that automatically reduces our costs. I think it's a no-brainer." It is fair to say that Costco's leadership is willing to take a lot of heat to make sure their people are well cared for. "We get a lot of pressure from the Wall Street analysts," said Galanti. "They seem to think we pay our people too well and that our profits would go up if we didn't. In the short-term . . . maybe, but longer term, we believe our strategy for hiring and retaining the best employees will help us to maximize earnings. To be honest, I don't mind taking that kind of heat, and neither does Jim Sinegal, our CEO."

One of the unquestionable influences at Costco is Sol Price. The philosophy that underlies Costco's success has a lot to do with Sol Price and the time that Jim Sinegal spent working for Price at Fed-Mart early in his career. Costco's values are a direct reflection of Sol Price's five-point philosophy of business.

It might be appropriate to add another of Sol Price's philosophies. He calls it the "intelligent loss of sales." Let's take a look at each of these principles.

When it comes to *obey the law,* Costco has a philosophy of avoiding the minimums. They tend to go beyond what is required by the law. "If we're building a new store and the code requires that we plant a specific number of trees, we go beyond that number. We want to make sure that the community understands up front that we respect their needs and desires," said Gal-

FIGURE 12.1 *Sol Price's Five-Point Philosophy of Business*

1. Obey the law.
2. Take care of our customers.
3. Take care of our employees.
4. Respect our suppliers, and, if we can accomplish 1 to 4, then . . .
5. Our shareholders will be rewarded.

anti. "We like to make sure that we go above and beyond just about every requirement our community values."

Take care of our customers is also a serious commitment at Costco. Not only is Costco committed to providing its members the lowest possible prices on the best quality items, the company offers its members what it terms an "unconditional, double guarantee." First, the company will fully refund a member's annual membership fee—100 percent—any time, no questions asked. Second, the company has an unquestioning return program for just about everything. Every product is 100 percent guaranteed. If you're not satisfied, simply return the item for a full refund. Neither a receipt nor the original packaging is required, and there's no time limit. The only exception to Costco's personal computer return policy was implemented in late 2003. "We had to look at that," said Galanti. "It seems that most computer systems are out of date within several months, so we can't justify taking a computer back after it's clearly obsolete. Historically, over one-half of the computers being returned were one to four years old. We changed the return policy to be "within six months;" that is still the most customer- friendly return policy in retail today—by at least five extra months. We've had good customer support on this. It's clear that they understood our dilemma."

Costco does control its profit margin on products. If a vendor approaches Costco with a special discount on an item, Costco passes the cost savings on to the customer. The company's leadership believes that such practices, although somewhat hidden from the customer, are best for all involved in the long run. "They may not know what we've done, but we do," said Galanti. "At some point, we believe that the customer begins to develop a high level of trust in us and in our integrity. A one-time profit opportunity, when compared with a lifelong customer relationship, is not a decision for us. We always choose our customers first; and we believe they appreciate that. And in the long run, our shareholders will benefit from that."

I have already alluded to the pressures that Costco's leadership experiences related to employee salaries and benefits. Costco believes that their

while still keeping prices low. At Costco, the mantra is high quality and low price. No exceptions.

Creating the Ultimate Customer Experience

You might think that Costco would get a lot of complaints from customers wanting larger product selections. That does not occur. The Costco customer apparently appreciates the value they can get and the integrity of the firm that stands behind each purchase. It might be said that the end result is a special relationship between the customer and this extremely smart company.

By now, it should be clear that Costco works hard to create the ultimate customer experience. It starts with low prices and high quality; it continues with motivated, caring employees; and it's driven home by a company that stands behind its products. Here's a story that illustrates the lengths that this exceptional company will go to make sure that every customer has the ultimate customer experience.

Early in its 20-year existence, Costco had warehouses on the West Coast plus two in Minneapolis/St. Paul, Minnesota, and one in Milwaukee, Wisconsin. In mid-1985, the firm's leadership determined that the three stores located in Minnesota and Wisconsin were losing more money than the company was making at their 19 West Coast locations. They concluded that their expansion to Minnesota and Wisconsin had been premature and concluded that they had to close the Midwest locations.

As a young, growing company, Costco had some decisions to make. They had nearly 100,000 members who had paid $25 each for shopping privileges at Costco. In some cases, the memberships had only a month of buying privileges left on them. In others, the members had just joined. Costco's response was to provide a full refund to all 100,000 people. It was not a prorated refund; each member got their $25 back in full.

As a side note, the company offered every employee a job at one of the company's other warehouse locations. Despite the difficulty of moving from Minnesota and Wisconsin to the Pacific Northwest, over 30 percent of the company's employees chose to transfer, and many are still with the company today.

Unsurprisingly, when the company was able to reenter the Minneapolis/ St. Paul market more than 15 years later, they were greeted with open arms and excited customers. That usually happens when a company provides the ultimate customer experience.

A Different Kind of Company

Like the other smart companies I studied, Costco executives have little time for self-importance or egos. Parking slots at corporate headquarters are allocated according to seniority, not position or title. That means that many of the 300 or so sheltered parking spaces go to the most tenured employees, irrespective of position or title, while less-tenured employees have to park uncovered and further away.

Corporate humility is also practiced at the company. Jim Sinegal, for example, had a wall knocked out of his office so that associates who were passing in the hallway would have open access to visit. The human resources group conducts what are called "caucus groups" with employees. The objective is to allow the employees, as much as is feasible, to design their own rules and workplace procedures.

If you call one of the senior executives of the firm, as I did in working on this story, you do not usually get an administrative person. The executive answers his or her own phone. That includes Jim Sinegal as well. The message to the Costco team is that there is always an open door and that input is always welcome, even at the highest levels of the firm.

Costco now has over 430 locations worldwide. Outside of the United States, the company has operations in Canada, the United Kingdom, Mexico, Korea, Taiwan, and Japan. Across the board, managers are expected to spend a great deal of their time in developing their employees. Although the company requires that at least 85 percent of all promotions come from internal candidates, the actual number is closer to 99 percent.

If you consider my three rules of strategy and leadership (maximize today, think and act out of the box, stay ahead of the curve), you will agree that Costco is one of those really smart companies. As such, it is reasonable to expect that this company will continue to grow and thrive. Costco's Corporate IQ assessment revealed that the company was extremely well matched in all 17 measured areas. It is designed to operate in the profit zone today and into the future.

DELL, INC.: ONE OF THE TEN
SMARTEST COMPANIES IN AMERICA

Imagine for a moment that you are the coach of a Super Bowl football team. Like other coaches, you take your team through all of the drills, and you prepare for anything that you could possibly face . . . almost. Imagine standing on the sideline, watching your team in the first quarter of the game, and suddenly realizing that something is seriously wrong.

You had noticed during the first few minutes of the game that the other team seemed to be executing slightly better than your team. But, ten minutes into the first quarter, after they were ahead by a touchdown, a realization hits you like rock in the pit of your stomach—the other team is significantly faster than your team. Not only is every player faster, but the team as a whole seems to adapt more quickly. As you watch, you realize that everything they are doing is simply much faster than what your team is doing. You quickly figure out that your team has little chance of beating a team that is so much faster.

Welcome to Dell, Inc. It is simply one of the fastest, most adaptive companies around. It is also a very complex organization. The abilities to be fast and complex combine to make the company a formidable competitor.

Dell, Inc.: A Customer's Perspective

I had written about Dell long before I had a personal experience with them. I think you will agree, after I finish telling you my story, that Dell's customers really like to do business with it. My customer experience began when I was given the task of finding a computer system for my church.

I had searched all the discount stores and other outlets and finally got around to looking at Dell. I was a little wary of having a computer shipped to me, because I usually like to pick out something at a store and take it home. But I'd found an ad by Dell that seemed to offer exactly what I wanted. I consulted with a couple of computer people whom I knew, and made the decision to call Dell, Inc.

I got through to a customer service person pretty quickly. I noticed that she had an ever so slight accent, so I asked her where she was. "India," she replied. I went ahead and told her what I wanted to order. The words were barely out of my mouth when she informed me that I was ordering the wrong system. She had been careful to make sure she understood exactly how we were going to use the system. She went on to explain a lot of technical things that I obviously did not understand but that she was kind enough to translate into simple language. "The system you are ordering is not suited for the application," she said. I braced myself for what I expected to be a bait-and-switch move to a much higher system.

Instead, she suggested that another model was much more suited to our application, and she explained all the differences. Then she suggested that I go ahead and order a network switch. Not counting the switch, the upgrade to the appropriate equipment was less than $75 per computer. I was a bit shocked at the amount because I was expecting it to be a lot more.

I ordered the system from Dell, only to find when it arrived that the switch was defective. Our administrative leader called Dell and explained the problem. They told us to expect a replacement part no later than the next day. It seems that there were some problems in getting the item from the warehouse to our location in Dallas. Imagine our surprise when a Dell employee arrived at the church that day. She had driven almost 200 miles to get the replacement part to us. Needless to say, I was impressed. That is why I decided I wanted to know more about this company.

Challenge Everything Processes

Some companies are not interested in challenging the status quo. In fact, at many companies, you can lose your job if you challenge the existing structure. Not so at Dell. In fact, the idea is to challenge everything to continually discover new and more efficient ways of doing things.

A few years ago, process reengineering was a hot topic. Some companies specialized in reengineering processes for clients. The only problem was that these companies were more about downsizing initiatives than they were about process cycle time reduction. For those who are not that familiar with process reengineering, it is a way of analyzing a process and cutting out unnecessary delays and activities. The average order-to-ship process that takes 60 days can usually be cut by 80 percent if the process is cleaned up. In the case of Dell, not only is every customer's order a custom-made system, but they can often ship on the same day they get the order and almost always within five business days. Compare that turnaround with that of the average competitor, who not only cannot ship an order in less than a couple of weeks, but lacks the ability to design the system precisely to the customer's

where the future will be. Tyson summed it up nicely: "We will go anywhere and create any product that makes sense, as long as it's adjacent and complementary to our current portfolio and represents profitable growth for our business. Right now, we want to maximize our existing portfolio of offerings, and at the same time, if we need to be different in the future, we want to be the first company that gets there."

Do You Really Care?

The Corporate IQ assessment involves 17 broad areas of the firm. During my visit with Lynn Tyson, I asked a pointed question: "Your Corporate IQ assessment indicated a small deficiency in an area called value of people." I went on to say that the smartest companies seemed to be obsessed with making sure that their people were recognized, valued, and appreciated. I was curious about this particular area, even though it was a slight blip on the assessment.

When I mentioned the issue to Lynn Tyson, she immediately agreed. She went on to explain what had happened. It seems that the technology meltdown of 2000 to 2001 had a significant impact on Dell. At first, the senior executive team seemed to be asking themselves, "What did we do wrong?" "That is when we realized that the industry had gone through a frame-breaking shift," said Tyson. "We immediately acknowledged the reality of the situation and, instead of being paralyzed by the downturn, we took swift action to refocus on our company's ability to aggressively recognize market opportunities and move toward them as rapidly as possible."

One of the benefits of working at Dell since its founding was the meteoric increases in the company's stock price. The disastrous events of the technology meltdown, paired with the impact of 9/11, hit every company in the United States if not the world. Dell was faced with what might be called its "last resort" approach for dealing with those changes. Dell had to downsize to match the new business reality. At the same time, the company continued its commitment to inspired excellence. A 2002 employee survey revealed that the downsizing and other pressures had pretty much deflated the level of inspiration in the organization. People were wondering if they really mattered anymore.

In the same way that the Dell organization attacks competitive challenges, they immediately launched a "winning culture" initiative to renew the company's spirit and communicate just how much each member of the

Dell team is valued and appreciated. By 2004, Dell had matched its external strategy changes with a coordinated program for communicating the importance of each individual in the firm. In a company with little tolerance for corporate egos, the message was loud and clear: "Our people make the profit, and we want them to understand how much we appreciate them, their hard work, and their focus on excellence." Smart companies view their people as being equally as important as their customers. Without the enthusiastic support of both, *inspired excellence* is little more than words on a page.

When the meltdown occurred, the immediate response of Dell's leadership was fast and meaningful. Dell was the first of the competitors in its segment to turn the corner. Dell's keen focus on balanced profitability in a low-growth environment was able to lead the company into a new and brighter future.

Perhaps Lynn Tyson explained it best. "We were the first movers when it came to changing our cost structure and reinvigorating our culture so we could continue to deliver the best value to our customers and employees. We learn fast. Once we implemented our product and people strategies, we were back on track."

Breaking the Mold Ethically

When looking at Dell, I asked for the opportunity to get a couple of different perspectives of the firm. Lynn Tyson provided wonderful perspectives on strategy. I was fortunate also to have the opportunity to visit with Thurmond Woodard, Dell's chief ethics officer and vice president of global diversity, who provided an inside perspective.

Smart companies understand that they can't be good in a few areas and be successful; they have to be good across the board. That is why the time with Thurmond Woodard was so valuable in providing a much broader look at the company.

I was pretty blunt in starting our interview: "How do you describe diversity?" Let me explain why I was so interested in his answer. We have all seen the word *diversity* used to justify a lot of things. When it comes to companies, I have observed that ill-conceived programs of preference can cause extensive damage. I'm all for diversity, but I believe we have to pair it with excellence to do the best for everyone involved.

"We believe that diversity is what drives our success," said Woodard, as he began to explain Dell's approach. "Diversity describes who we are as people. If we are to be an innovative company that challenges the future, we have to be able to not only tolerate people who are different, but we need to be able to encourage them. Diversity is not about race or gender; it's about attitudes and abilities."

I purposely pressed him a bit further on this issue. He began talking about the "Soul of Dell" and how those values and principles drive everything the company does. The word *soul* is often used to describe the inner being of a person. In this case, it is used to describe the stuff of which Dell is composed. The "Soul of Dell" is more than a simple phrase; it is a well-conceived document that covers every aspect of what the company does. From unquestionable integrity, to people relationships, the community, and customers, Dell uses its "Soul of Dell" as a strategic compass to guide everything it does.

Two statements in the "Soul of Dell" document captured my attention. Here is the first.

> At Dell, we value and are committed to: Customers, the Dell Team, Direct Relationships, Global Citizenship, and Winning.

It is important to note that the company philosophy recognizes the value of balance between the organization, its team members, the community, and, of course, the firm's *raison d'etre*—winning! In our discussion, Woodard talked a lot about excellence. Woodard took that idea of winning to his view of diversity. He explained that the company's objective was to create a workplace in which every member of the team believed that they had the freedom to make a difference. I got a kick out of his comments on this topic.

> *"We want to access talent. We don't care about the package."*
> —Thurmond Woodard

History is filled with instances in which really bright people experienced difficulty because they were different. Albert Einstein apparently did not do well in math as a young child. Walt Disney was fired by a newspaper because his boss felt he was not a good idea man. Enrico Caruso's parents were urged to send him to engineering school, because, according to his voice teacher, he "has no voice at all." Smart companies understand that really talented people come wrapped in all kinds of packages. They also realize that great companies find ways to discover the genius in everyone they hire. Wouldn't you love to work for a company that does that? Maybe that's why so many of the smart companies have a lot more "smart applicants" than their counterparts.

Take a Stand!

This word is loaded with meaning: *Enron.* Most remember the news reports of financial misrepresentation and tragic losses by stockholders as well as employees of this troubled company. One of the things I have found in the smartest companies might appear on the surface as a dichotomy. On one hand, there is a preoccupation with creativity and challenging everything. On the other, there are unquestionable standards of practice and ethical behavior.

When you think about it, that dual focus makes sense. If you as a manager encourage your people to be risk takers who engage in creatively discovering the future, they will make some mistakes. At the same time, if no ethical standard supports the risk-taking employee, all creative activity will cease. The highest of ethical standards creates the highest levels of trust. That applies to employees, vendors, stockholders, and customers. That's another way of saying that high ethical standards go straight to the bottom line.

Uncompromised Integrity

Another thing that became clear during my discussion with Thurmond Woodard relates to the corporate attitude regarding any breach of ethics. Integrity is the standard in every aspect of an employee's life at the company, regardless of their position. Dealings with subordinates, peers, vendors, and customers are expected to be of the highest ethical nature. "If all else fails," says Woodard, "do the right thing."

Doing the right thing is in the very fiber of Dell. It's part of their corporate DNA. The same is true of the "Soul of Dell" principles and practices. From their first day on the job until they retire, every member of the team is reminded of the standards by which the firm operates. The good news is, good people want to work for a company with those standards as minimums.

SMART BUSINESS

It seems fashionable today to take pot shots at companies that take morality seriously. Some are tempted to criticize companies with high levels of employee commitment. The leaders of companies that commit to taking a moral, ethical approach in managing their company are willing to take the heat because it is simply the right thing to do. Smart companies are aggressive, they are adaptive, and they insist on high levels of corporate character. That must be why some of the world's most profitable companies are also quite smart.

Chapter

13

MEASURING SUCCESS

Smart companies are different from their lesser counterparts. In every case, smart companies have a well-established system of accountability. If I were to single out the one single flaw in management thinking that does the most to destroy companies, it is an all too common misunderstanding of accountability. The old management approach makes managers accountable for results. The problem is, it fails to make managers accountable for the behaviors that produce sustained success.

Let me put it another way: if high performance goals are the only standard you establish, you leave managers free to use "whatever means necessary" to reach them. You may win a few battles with that approach, but ultimately you will lose the war.

When you look at Corporate IQ, you discover that measuring, or accountability, means focusing on the behaviors that produce high levels of achievement, not looking only at the outcomes or goals. Let us look at just one area that is a consistent problem at companies that I have studied: leadership style. Leadership style is discussed in Chapter 7 on organization. You probably remember that a level 1 leadership style is highly controlling, while a level 5 leadership style is highly empowering and charismatic. Simply put, the higher the competitive index, the competitive environment or context becomes more competitive with a higher rate of speed (of change). Highly controlling management can kill a company in a competitive context that involves high rates of change and high levels of complexity.

Excellence or extremely high standards of performance are the norm in smart companies. To make sure that the company is capable of achieving those goals, the managers are accountable for how they treat subordinates. Earlier, I talked a lot about the significance principle. When it comes to leadership, the significance principle is involved on both sides of the transaction. On one side, managers are often tempted to build their personal significance by deriving it from those they supervise. Although such "self-esteem" is false, some managers are so psychologically needy that they think nothing of demanding that subordinates engage in rituals like calling them "mister" or forcing them to endure public rages over a missed goal.

The other side of the significance transaction involves the subordinate. I happen to believe that most people really have a desire to be involved in excellence. At the same time, if they are discounted and publicly humiliated, most people will give little more than their manager demands. The result is significant underutilization of the company's talent.

It makes a lot of sense to make managers accountable for how they treat their subordinates. When combined with an expectation of excellence, a commitment to recognize, appreciate, and value subordinates can drive an organization to new levels of achievement. Yes, the idea is simple, but as I said, a lot of managers are more interested in having their egos stroked than in the long-term success of the firm.

When you compare the approaches of smart managers with those of other managers, you begin to discover the real reasons behind corporate success and failure. It should be abundantly clear by now that how managers think has everything to do with how they behave. As a result, how managers think and how they behave directly impacts the companies that they lead. I have written a lot about success in this book, but now I will pay attention briefly to failures. Low-performing managers often do not stick around to experience the results of their misdeeds. That does not change the reality of their outcomes. Highly ineffective managers can and do obtain short-term improvement. The only problem is, when they leave, nothing but devastation is left behind. Just to make sure you know how to spot one of these people, I have prepared a list (see Figure 13.1).

We can all identify with the preceding list. The truth is there are a lot of people who seem to think that such behaviors are necessary if one is to be a successful manager. Reality reveals otherwise. As you consider the leaders of each of the top ten smartest companies, it is clear that they are the exact opposite. I call those exceptional leaders "level five leaders." I'll briefly explain the concept.

FIGURE 13.1 *The Fifteen Stupid Habits of Highly Ineffective Managers*

1. They believe that management is all about controlling others.
2. They think the latest fad will save their company.
3. They think that downsizing is a strategy.
4. They are obsessed with what the firm used to be (historic competencies).
5. They demand respect (instead of earning it).
6. They sacrifice anything or anyone to make their quarterly numbers.
7. They take credit for the work of others.
8. They hire and promote compliant people.
9. They are people of intrigue and avoid transparency at all costs.
10. They view integrity as less important than results.
11. They value political skill in people as more important than performance and productivity.
12. They insist on being called "mister" or another, similar title.
13. Their door is never open.
14. They view humility as a sign of weakness.
15. They have contempt for subordinates.

LEVEL FIVE LEADERS

H. Igor Ansoff, the strategist who originated the idea of evaluating context and organizations on a five-point scale, must be credited with laying the foundation for what I call "level five leadership."[1] In his early work, he talked a lot about the importance of leaders who are charismatic as well as empowering. Ansoff believed that such leaders were critically important to firms that were operating in environments with competitive indexes in the four to five range (thus, "level five leaders"). As a result of his work as well as my own, I would like to share what I believe are the characteristics and beliefs of level five leaders.

- Having humility
- Having integrity
- Inspirational
- Empowering
- Defining success in terms of their people's accomplishments
- Having excellence as their minimum standard
- Proactive listening
- Seeking first the best for others and believing that profits will come as a result

It does not take long to figure out that level five leaders have little tolerance for self-absorption and egocentric behavior. They are unwilling to build their own success at the expense of others. Let's look at one of these exceptional people.

BARBARA MEDLIN: LEVEL FIVE LEADERSHIP

Barbara Medlin is responsible for the national marketing effort of a large financial institution. Over the past few years, I have had the opportunity to observe her personally in a number of different circumstances. I became so intrigued with just how gifted she is as a manager; I asked a number of her subordinates and peers to send me e-mails that describe how she leads.

My first exposure to Medlin was when her organization was undergoing a major reorganization. Needless to say, she was surrounded by unhappy people. I discovered that Medlin operates on a personal philosophy of "recognize the best and avoid the rest." That principle involves focusing on the positive aspects of a situation you cannot control and avoiding the negatives. I am sure that Medlin, as did others in her organization, disagreed with at least a few of the decisions that were made. Yet, she consistently chose to avoid getting on the negative bandwagon. When negatives were brought up, Medlin consistently focused on the best.

We have all met people who were unable or unwilling to recognize unproductive situations. Medlin is not one of those people. Medlin is realistic when it comes to recognizing what she can change and what she cannot. The result is that she avoids the negative rut that some get into. Medlin chooses to focus on being the best she can be in areas where she can affect the outcome. Rather than perpetuating the unavoidable negativism of a situation, she chooses to use "focus on the best" to keep her people focused and productive.

Not surprisingly, the e-mails I got from Medlin's subordinates were extremely positive. In fact, if you look at the eight characteristics of level five leaders, they generally describe exactly how her associates and her subordinates feel about her leadership style. One very bright subordinate made a telling comment: "She encourages her people."

Unsurprisingly, people enjoy being a part of Medlin's organization. This is characteristic of what happens to level five leaders. At most companies, it is not unusual to find that there are waiting lists of internal applicants who want to work for a level five leader. After all, who wouldn't want to work for someone like a Barbara Medlin?

Level five leaders hold themselves as well as others accountable for how people are recognized, valued, and appreciated. One of the companies that seems to maintain a nice balance between excellence and how it values employees is Microsoft. The company was established on the idea of "getting to the future first," so it should be no surprise that the company continues to focus on that issue. Staying ahead of the curve is a Microsoft mantra. The company's leadership understands that its people and its leaders must work together to accomplish that goal. That is why the company has continued to do extremely well over the years.

MICROSOFT: ONE OF THE TEN SMARTEST COMPANIES IN AMERICA

When you think about Microsoft, it's natural to think about Bill Gates. One of the things I wanted to do in this book was to get an internal view of the firm. I asked people who were way down in the middle of the firm's management structure to talk about things like . . . Bill Gates. More than that, I wanted an insider's perspective on how the firm does business.

Before I selected Microsoft for this book, I conducted a Corporate IQ assessment on the firm. Through a few contacts who trusted my motives, I was able to get the assessment completed. Let me begin by saying that Microsoft's Corporate IQ was extremely high. Obviously, that's one of the reasons that they were selected as one of the top ten smartest companies in America. They measured out as having aggressive strategies, a highly adaptive organization, and the corporate character to go with it. They are truly a well-balanced company. With a Corporate IQ in the top tier, I expect Microsoft to continue to show sustained, high earnings.

You may remember that earlier, I suggested that my three rules of strategy are, "Maximize today, think and act out of the box, and stay ahead of the curve." That is exactly what Microsoft does exceedingly well. I had the opportunity to spend some time with one of those who had completed the Corporate IQ assessment on Microsoft. I would like for him to remain anonymous, so I will simply call him "John."

One of the first things I asked him was what role Bill Gates now plays in the company. "He's the chairman and the chief technology architect," said John. "But his love and his skill are in the latter role of chief technology architect." John went on to say that, even from way down in the firm, it was clear that Gates's role as the creative engine of the firm had not changed since its inception. He went on to say that Gates and Steve Ballmer (CEO) are great at sticking to their respective roles. "Ballmer runs the company," said John.

I asked John to talk about the internal workings of the company. John explained that the Microsoft culture is different from that of most other companies. "If you come to work at Microsoft and you do extremely well in every area of your job, that means you've met the minimums," said John. John expanded on the idea by explaining that every member of the Microsoft team was expected to look beyond the obvious and to try to discover the exceptional. "It's all about 'empowered excellence.'" He went on to explain that managers tend to avoid being controlling or directive. Instead, they point you in a direction, and it's your job to figure out how to get there.

The Secret Weapon

I asked John if he could identify the one real key to the company's success. Without even blinking, he said, "People." If you are like me, you have become jaded by that saying over the years. I quickly discovered, however, that John was extremely serious about his idea. John wanted me to understand just how the company is so radically different from most others. John, incidentally, had worked at a number of well-known organizations prior to joining Microsoft. He felt that I needed to understand what the average prospective employee had to go through to get a job with the firm. Hiring processes are different for various areas of the company; in John's area, a lot of emphasis was placed on the technical components of the job.

He explained that the first step for his area was a technical interview—a little like running a gauntlet, according to John. The applicant would spend 30 minutes on the phone in a fast-paced discussion of the various technical issues involved in the job. If you get through the short technical interview, then you get to go through the long technical interview. That interview, one-and-one-half hours on the phone, is a bit on the grueling side, according to John. If the applicant is fortunate enough to get through the second interview, then they get to visit with an interview panel. The interview panel is composed of two managers and two others who work in the job area that the applicant is pursuing. Incidentally, neither of the managers in that interview is the hiring manager.

The third interview is a real switch from the first two. The applicant is given a lot of scenarios and asked to comment on how they would solve a problem. This exercise challenges the logic and thinking skills of the applicant. "What we are looking for in the third interview," said John, "is to see if we can evaluate the critical thinking skills of the applicant. Critical thinking is a core skill requirement in our culture."

If the applicant does well enough on the third interview, there is a fourth interview. That interview is with the actual hiring manager. If the applicant is successful in that interview, then and only then can they be offered a job.

John went on to explain that the interviews are each carefully designed to get an in-depth understanding of the applicant. "We spend a great deal of time to make sure that we get the very best people," said John. John explained that the purpose of the interviews, in addition to examining qualifications, was to find out if the applicant was someone with the desire and ability to be special. He talked about how his particular division described that special attribute with the word *wow!* "I don't know how to define that word, except to say that we are looking for something in an applicant that is beyond the job and is really impressive," he said. "It's difficult to describe, but when you find someone with 'wow,' you know it." Like most exceptional companies, Microsoft hires approximately 1 in 400 applicants.

The applicant interview process at Microsoft is complemented by the employee evaluation process. John explained that the company uses a technique called "stacking" in their evaluation and rewards process. Those who rank toward the bottom with respect to their peers receive little or no salary increases or bonuses. Those who rank in the middle receive limited increases. "We're unashamedly a meritocracy," said John. "The people who contribute the most get the lion's share of the incentives. It's just that simple."

Create Your Own Future

One interesting thing that John talked about was just how much emphasis was placed on creativity. "It's easier to get $1 million than it is to add one new person to your headcount," said John. John went on to explain that Microsoft encourages its people to have ideas. He explained that in its culture, everyone is viewed as important, and anyone who had a desire to create a new product or cut costs is always given an opportunity to present their case.

All of this may contribute to the fact that the turnover at Microsoft is extremely low. People simply do not want to leave. John suggested that a high percentage of those who do leave each year are probably retirees instead of those who go to another company.

Why Does Microsoft Continue to Win?

I have written a lot about how companies must combine aggressive strategy and a highly adaptive organization. As luck would have it, as I was starting to write this paragraph, my phone rang. It was an individual for whom I will be doing a strategy session later in the month. It turns out that he had done some work within Microsoft a few years ago. Here's what he said about the firm: "They are the most proactive change organization I have ever seen. If you point them a direction, they are already on the way before anything else is said. They are a phenomenally aggressive, adaptive organization."

That is why Microsoft continues to win. In addition to an aggressive strategic approach and a highly adaptive organization, the firm has strong organizational character. Without high levels of integrity to create exceptional trust among all members of the Microsoft team, the firm would be unable to sustain itself. Microsoft's culture has that level of trust, and it probably will continue to be one of the smartest companies in America.

Companies like Microsoft clearly must be involved in a continual process of reinventing themselves. But what about those companies that are not involved in technology and the rapid churn that goes along with competing in those types of competitive segments? Does it make sense for them to reinvent themselves continually? If you are one of the "top ten smartest companies in America," the answer is yes.

A.G. Edwards is an NYSE traded company. It also has been around for over 100 years. Like other smart companies, A.G. Edwards is sustained by its commitment to extremely high levels of corporate character. That may be why the company also has an innovative and customercentric strategy.

A.G. EDWARDS: ONE OF THE TEN SMARTEST COMPANIES IN AMERICA

Smart companies appear to do a lot of things that make little sense to outsiders. In an industry known for its high turnover, A.G. Edwards spends a lot of money on training and coaching its new financial consultants. While some companies are content to live with a harsh, survival-of-the-fittest approach, smart companies spend a lot of effort on finding good people and then keeping them.

A few years ago, I was asked to develop a benchmark for evaluating training organizations. One tool that I discovered was a methodology for computing the return on investment of the dollars spent on training. What I discovered was astounding. Few, if any, companies had any meaningful way of measuring the bottom-line value of their training programs. Not surprisingly, companies often slash their training programs with little consideration of the impact of such cuts. Often, the negative outcome of such cuts shows up months or even years later.

Appropriate training impacts the bottom line. One of the first discoveries I made about A.G. Edwards is that they continually assess their "training ROI" and have a real appreciation for great training's contribution to corporate performance. In fact, the firm's chairman and chief executive officer, Robert L. Bagby, views training and ongoing professional development as cornerstones of his corporate strategy. The company also stays in touch with recent trainees with coaching and additional course offerings after they complete the firm's formal training program. Ironically, at most companies, little attention is paid to the effectiveness of an employee's training once they get back to their jobs. Of course, on the job is the most important place to measure training. By engaging in a proactive coaching program for their financial consultants, A.G. Edwards has been able to keep its turnover significantly lower than that of its industry counterparts, resulting in increased profit.[2]

I had the opportunity to visit with Donnis L. Casey, executive vice president of the firm, to discuss some of these issues. She suggested that one of the core values that has historically contributed to the success of A.G. Edwards is its customer commitment. "Our approach is to focus on our clients' needs, believing that if we do what's best for the client, the profits will follow," she said. She went on to explain that the company expects their consultants to work for their clients, and that means there are never special incentives to sell the latest stock or bond deal.

A Sustainable Difference

A.G. Edwards is one of the few companies that has been included in all seven editions of *Fortune's* list of "The 100 Best Companies to Work for in

America." Having spent a number of years in financial institutions myself, I found that a bit surprising. The highly regulated nature of most financial institutions usually creates management teams that focus on compliance and control. That usually results in inflexible cultures and controlling management, and rarely is such a place one of the "best to work for" companies. But A.G. Edwards is different.

Founded in 1887 by General Albert Gallatin Edwards, the company has a rich history. Long before it was fashionable, the leadership at A.G. Edwards made "the importance of the client" an integral part of its organizational strategy and culture. You may recognize a hint of the golden rule in a statement made in 1967 by former chairman and CEO Ben Edwards III, the great-grandson of the firm's founder:

> Our purpose is to furnish financial services of value to our clients. We should act as their agents, putting their interests before our own.

> We are confident that if we do our jobs well and give value for what we charge, not only will mutual trust and respect develop, but satisfaction and a fair reward will result.

This statement has become the foundation for the mission statement of the firm, and current CEO Bob Bagby makes sure its ideals carry on. Interviews with executives from the "top ten smartest companies in America" reveal that the Golden Rule is a standard of behavior at almost every company. Companies that act in that manner are capable of creating the ultimate customer experience on a consistent basis.

I think it is important for you to understand how this plays out in the operation of the company. A.G. Edwards comes by its client-first philosophy honestly. Just prior to the Great Depression, a lot of brokerage houses began allowing clients to have large margin accounts. That meant that a client might be able to buy $1 million of stock but only put up a small percentage in actual cash. The brokerage firm would loan the balance on what is called "margin."

A.G. Edwards's leadership did not believe that such leveraging was in the best interest of either its clients or the company. That is one of the reasons why they came through the Depression so well. In fact, the largest loss sustained by any A.G. Edwards client during the great depression was a $5,000 loss on a $1 million portfolio.

The Inverted Pyramid . . . Again

I have to confess that I made an interesting discovery as I did the research and interviews for this book. What I discovered was that the smartest companies had a lot more in common than a high Corporate IQ. For example, almost all founded their decisions on a version of the Golden Rule: "Do unto others as you would have them do unto you." Another almost universal practice among the smart companies was their use of the inverted pyramid to describe their organizational focus.

The idea of the inverted pyramid reverses the common view of an organization: having the customers at the bottom level of the pyramid, the employees above them, managers above them, and the executives at the pyramid's peak. Smart companies invert that hierarchy of importance. That is, the customers and the employees are at the top (now inverted, because there are a lot more employees and customers than managers), the managers are in the middle, and the executives are at the bottom. Another thing I have observed at the smart companies is that, when the pyramid is presented in its normal mode with the senior executives at the top, the message is not power; rather, it is responsibility.

When you put all of this together, it means that the importance ranking in smarter companies looks like this:

1. Customers and employees (shareholders)
2. Managers
3. Executives

Some choose to put the shareholders in that picture as well. They will generally rank shareholders as more important than executives. The bottom line is that smart companies believe that by ranking customers and employees as the most important aspects of their business model, the rest of the parties will experience maximum return.

The other side of the coin is the responsibility ranking. That looks like the traditional pyramid with the executives and shareholders at the top. That pyramid describes where the responsibility lies for keeping the importance pyramid intact. In other words, the senior executives are responsible for keeping the customers and the employees at the top of the "importance list" so that organizational performance is maximized.

"That's exactly where we are," Bagby told me, when I had a chance to visit with him. "Our starting point is client- and employee-centric." He went on to explain that the inverted pyramid and the Golden Rule are the driving forces behind everything that the company does.

At some securities firms, every area of the firm is a profit center. That means that the bond division must make a profit, then the broker must also make a profit when the customer buys a bond. The result is that customers can pay a lot of mark-ups based on the internal processes of the company. Another practice at some securities firms is even more customer-averse. At some companies, the decision is made to push a specific bond, stock, or service. Each broker is then given a quota of those specific items to sell. The conflict between customer needs and corporate directives is clear.

In A.G. Edwards's processes, such practices are not allowed. In fact, in true inverted pyramid tradition, the financial consultants (the A.G. Edwards title for all its brokers) can select products based on their perception of their clients' needs. There is a saying: "He who holds the gold makes the rules." It might be said that at this company, the "gold" is the clients, and they make the rules.

That also translates into a long-term investment philosophy geared toward client success rather than toward following hot leads and rumors, a practice that can frequently work against clients. "We have a bit of an advantage in some ways," said Bagby. "Being in St. Louis (the corporate headquarters for A.G. Edwards) allows us to avoid the herd mentality that sometimes takes over brokerage firms in New York." He went on to say that, in the same way that the company expects their financial consultants to approach their clients' needs with a long term view, the same is true of the company's philosophy of doing business. "We take the approach that, if it's not good for our client, it's not good for us," Bagby said. "That keeps our focus on stable, long-term opportunities. Sure, you might get lucky chasing a hot stock every once in a while, but our observation has been that in the long run, you could lose a lot of your clients' money that way."

It's All About Philosophy

You will recall that I have spent a lot of time throughout this book talking about how management is a philosophy. In my interviews, the continual reference to "our philosophy" caught my attention. I truly believe that how managers think is how they act. Few would disagree with that. As I listened to Bob Bagby and others, it became clear to me that A.G. Edwards, like the other smart companies featured in this book, makes sure that everyone involved with the firm understands the company's philosophy of business.

One of the ways that plays out occurs during the first day a new employee is with the company. New hires are exposed to people from every area of the firm. Not surprisingly, there is a lot of talk about the principles and practices that drive business activity. By the end of their first day on the job, every new employee understands that a common philosophy guides the people of A.G. Edwards. To make sure that each new hire understands the broad nature of this commitment, they are invited to Bob Bagby's office and, if he is in town, visit with him during their tour of the firm's home office. Bagby wants new employees to understand that putting clients first is not just talk; it is the first rule of everything that they do.

The Grid

OCS (Officer's Candidate School) is where prospective officers in the U.S. Army have gone for years to obtain their initial training to become an officer. For those who have been through such a program, it is an experience that they will never forget. Some may remember the grueling physical demands of the course. But none will forget its mental demands. The OCS staff purposely wears the candidates down physically, creates overwhelming pressure as well as confusion, and then puts the candidates into a decision-making situation.

The military has learned that candidates who fare well in such demanding simulations will usually do well when they are confronted with real-world situations on the battlefield. In some ways, that describes a training program that A.G. Edwards uses called The Grid, a program created and updated by Robert R. Blake.

A.G. Edwards likes for its management personnel to go through this one-week leadership program. It's not your typical "one week in a classroom and fill out a smile sheet" type of class. The class features a full week of decision-making activities covering a variety of scenarios. Managers are asked to participate in group activities that simulate some of the challenges that they encounter when they work collaboratively in their day-to-day activities. It's all about people, clients, ethics, and results philosophy. At the end of the week, the managers apply the company's philosophy of business as groups present their thoughts and ideas on areas of improvement to the firm's executive leadership team—including CEO Bob Bagby.

"It's all about openness, teamwork, and communication," says Donnis Casey. "Each manager spends a great deal of time in understanding his or her management style. It's a personal growth experience that not only helps each person understand himself or herself better, but also instills a sense of integrity in communication. The Grid calls that 'candor.'" Casey added that outsiders often do not believe it when they hear stories of how free people are to express their views within the company. "Candor is very important in our business," she said, "not only in our internal communications among employees but also when we're dealing with our clients."

One of the most important things at A.G. Edwards is its overall leadership philosophy. It is best summed up by the following list:

- Honesty
- The Golden Rule
- Open door
- Candor (teamwork)

As with the other smart companies, the A.G. Edwards philosophy is founded on honesty. As a company that values innovation by every team member, the company's leadership recognizes the critical relationship between creative excellence, honesty, and trust. They also believe that their commitment to integrity in dealing with associates will be passed along in their relationships with clients.

You will note that having an open door is an important philosophy at the company. That means if someone wants to visit with Bob Bagby, there are several ways to do so. That same reality is played out every day in every office in the company. At the same time, every one of the company's 16,000 people understands that they are the key to sustaining the firm's history of high ethical standards and innovation. The open door policy is one avenue that every member of that team has to accomplish those objectives.

A lot of people have the impression that empowerment is tantamount to having managers sitting around a campfire together singing "Kumbaya" in harmony. I love that song, but at the same time, I do not think that is an accurate picture of empowerment at most companies. Smart companies will generally practice "empowered excellence." Empowered excellence conveys the idea of a joint commitment to excellence in the context of personal responsibility.

At A.G. Edwards, it translates into a leadership philosophy that I would call "candor coaching." It's the idea of using honesty and candor to help subordinates to be more successful. It goes without saying that honesty has to be at the foundation of any leader's relationship with subordinates. In using a candor coaching approach, the team member is provided a clear understanding of performance-related issues. At the same time, rather than taking a demeaning or demanding approach, the leader is expected to coach the team member to excellence. As with other smart organizations, A.G. Edwards does not like to be wrong when hiring people. Candor coaching is a proactive, positive approach for making sure that the company keeps its people.

The Proof Is in the Pudding

A lot of companies talk about how they value their people. In a number of cases, they do not practice what they preach. Often, the result is short tenure and high turnover. That's why "the proof's in the pudding" is a great approach to discovering if companies walk the talk.

As mentioned previously, A.G. Edwards has one of the lowest turnover rates among financial consultants among financial services companies. In addition, the firm strives to ensure that its people are valued, appreciated, and recognized in a variety of ways. A.G. Edwards takes a share-the-wealth approach with all team members. All full-time and part-time employees get 5 percent of their salary as a company contribution to their 401(k). That occurs whether the employee contributes or not. Additionally, full-time and part-time employees also get annual profit sharing contributions based on the company's overall performance.

The company also has a philosophy of promoting from within. People are encouraged to gain a greater understanding of all aspects of the firm's business, and in some cases, that attitude has allowed employees to take advantage of a broad range of opportunities.

Another factor that underlies the success of the company is RAVE leadership. You will remember from Chapter 10 that RAVE means recognize, appreciate, and value employees, while expecting excellence from yourself as well as every member of your team. You will also remember that RAVE plays a major role in company performance by confirming the significance or value of an individual. Margaret Welch, the director of public relations, told me a personal story about what happened to her one day at A.G. Edwards that illustrates just how this company's leadership feels about confirming the value of its people.

"Actually there were two situations that really made an impact on me," Welch said. "The first came at the conclusion of our recent launch of a new branding initiative. When we finished the project, our entire department was treated to a pizza party that was attended by several members of our executive team." She went on to tell about her tenth anniversary with the company. Her coworkers had created a video that detailed a lot of Welch's time at A.G. Edwards. There was a lot of good-natured fun in the comments from her coworkers, but there was recognition for her contributions as well. "Imagine my surprise," Welch said, "when I heard a familiar voice behind me laughing at all the funny videotaped barbs of my coworkers, and there was Bob Bagby . . . there to show his appreciation as well. Money doesn't produce the attitude I have for this company and our people. That kind of care and recognition does."

Transparent Leadership

I often find that outsiders have problems believing that any company could run like A.G. Edwards and the other smart companies that I have cited in this book. They are unable to believe simply because they have never been treated that well. Bob Bagby often says, "Our brand is our people, and our product is our knowledge." For that statement to be true, the entire leadership team of A.G. Edwards has to live that reality in everything that they do. They have to lead with high standards of ethical conduct. The bottom line of that type of leadership is simply, "What you see is what you get."

You do not have to look very far to find people who want to take pot shots at companies that are run by those types of leaders. Not only do they not believe that what they see is true, they often have a bit of contempt for such companies because of their ethical standards and how they treat their people. Regardless, if you ask the people who work for companies like A.G. Edwards, you will find that they want to work there simply because of the transparency, the integrity, and the leadership of those who guide such organizations.

Bob Bagby: A Leader Who Serves

Bob Bagby views his job as that of serving others. The open door to his office is just one way that he sends that important message. Another way is his monthly broadcasts on A.G. Edwards's internal radio network. The

16,000 plus people of A.G. Edwards who work around the country can tune into the network, obtain a CD of the broadcast after it airs, or listen via the firm's intranet. Usually, the program starts out with a few remarks from Bagby, but then the floor is open for discussion. During the program, people have the opportunity to ask pressing questions without being identified.

Although he cannot always be face-to-face with all of the people in the company, Bagby uses this open exchange of ideas to make sure that the concerns of the firm's employees are heard and that action is taken when and where appropriate. Rather than being a one-way broadcast, this exchange between a CEO and his employees is just one way that Bob Bagby lives the principle of leading through service. "I believe the bottom line is that the profits of a company start with your people," Bagby said. He went on to explain the basics that are the focus of the organization.

- Branding: the A.G. Edwards people
- The Product: knowledge

"We're a relationship company," Bagby said. "Our job is to focus on our people, and their job is to focus on the client. That's why we spend a lot of time training our employees, so that they are able to provide knowledge."

A.G. Edwards is serious about taking care of the client. For example, the firm's research analysts are compensated, in part, based on the performance of their recommendations, which motivates them to keep the client's best interests in mind at all times. "They get their incentives for recommending securities that perform well," Bagby said, "and we believe that never puts them in conflict with the client." He went on to explain that, unlike many in the securities industry, A.G. Edwards is not in a lot of other businesses, such as owning their own bank. That means that they have to pay the bills by doing well in the securities industry.

Bob Bagby believes in communication. Each month, he has a special luncheon with people from each division. He said that he often gets some tremendous ideas from those luncheons. He went on to talk about how the firm was involved in a long-term process to change its technology capabilities radically. Bagby believes that the candor and communication that occurs within the firm is one of the keys to the highly innovative nature of the company.

During our conversation, Bagby spent a lot of time talking about ethics. One of the basic rules that everyone is expected to operate on is always to put the customer first. "We never put ourselves in a conflict position," Bagby said. "That's why our financial consultants are free to design a portfolio that is clearly the best for their client. As long as they deal with integrity and put the client first, we are happy."

Bob Bagby's final comment related to the company's training and the importance of maintaining a dynamic curriculum—better known as A.G. Edwards University—that reflects the growing needs of the firm's clients. He made it clear that they believe in continual training. "We train-train-train," Bagby said. He went on to discuss the company's new 200,000-square-foot learning center that houses A.G. Edwards University. Bagby believes that success is a simple formula: "First you hire and train the best people. Second, you make sure that your people have every tool they need to make money for their clients. Third, you continue to keep your people at the top by continuing to educate them."

THE ULTIMATE MOTIVATOR

At A.G. Edwards, the standard is excellence. Everyone is expected to commit to excellence in everything that they do, but they are also accountable for the work they do. Excellence begins with integrity in all dealings, especially with clients. It's the glue that creates that inseparable bond between client, company, and employees.

At companies where the significance principle is applied, the managers as well as their subordinates are highly motivated. They want to go above and beyond, because those who lead them continually go above and beyond on their behalf. The result is openness, organizational flexibility, and speed that allow the company to take advantage of opportunities as they emerge.

That "people make the profit" is true, as one of our CEOs said during an interview. That reality can propel a company to greatness and sustain it at the highest levels. The philosophy drives those who are responsible for leading at the ten smartest companies in America.

14

WHAT'S YOUR CORPORATE IQ?

Smart leaders understand that the key to sustainable performance is their ability to keep the organization firmly planted in the profit zone. In my discussions of Corporate IQ to this point, I have purposely tried to avoid involving the reader in technical information. At the same time, I believe that you need to understand how Corporate IQ is calculated and also how to use it to change your organization. It might be appropriate to offer a refresher from Chapter 6: the organization is made up of three distinct areas:

1. Strategy defines the aggressive capabilities of the firm.
2. Organization describes the adaptive capabilities of the firm.
3. Character describes the foundations upon which the company operates.

The idea is not simple, but once it grabs your mind, you really will not be able to think in any other way. It is critically important to remember that the first two areas, *strategy* and *organization,* are context-dependent. The third, *character* is not. Character is critical regardless of the competitive context. Let's look at each area again to make sure that the concepts are clear.

Competitor Index

All strategy work must have, as its starting point, a clear profile of what competitors will be doing in the future. I do not want to discuss in too great detail how competitor behavior is predicted, except to say that by using the charts in Chapter 4, it is possible to examine future competitive behavior systematically, then develop an understanding of the future competitive index in your segment. Again, competitive index (or competitor index—I use them interchangeably) is an application of systems thinking. In the consulting arena, we use three different views of the future to arrive at our final index: internal managers of the client company (almost always flawed), the view obtained from relevant literature and research, and the view of a panel of experts. Once the three views are obtained, each is evaluated, and a final determination of the future competitive index is calculated. The accuracy of this process has been confirmed in over 100 major studies in the past 12 years.

Once you understand that the competitive index provides a clear description of how competitors will behave in the future, the entire process becomes extremely clear. If I understand that my competitors will be operating at a competitive index of 4.2, I immediately know that they will be highly aggressive in the creation of new products and that they will be devoting substantial assets to highly aggressive marketing activities. It also follows that, as the leader of a firm that is competing in that specific context, my company has little chance of doing well if I do not creatively match my organization to the competitors' strategies. If I fail to respond, the creative destruction efforts of the competitors will eliminate my company. Again, strategy and organization must match context. Let's briefly review how the entire process works.

Figure 14.1, "The Profit Zone," presents the concept in a simplistic manner, but at the same time, it reveals how we can paint mental pictures of the firm. This is the same graphic that I presented in Chapter 6 to explain Corporate IQ. Notice that, in the example, the firm's competitors will be operating at a competitive index of level 4.0. That's a pretty competitive environment, with very high levels of chaos (unpredictability), and the competitors will be highly creative as well as highly aggressive marketers. The chart indicates that the profit zone for our company is between 3.5 and 4.5. Anything outside of that area will impact future profit.

Again, observe what we are doing. First we measure the future competitors' behavior on a five-point scale. Then we measure our current company on a five-point scale. Then, we compare the two to see if we are already in the profit zone. The further away from the competitive index we are, the

FIGURE 14.1   *The Profit Zone*

	1	2	3	4	5
Strategy	Slow follower	Follower	Aggressive	Very aggressive	Take no prisoners
Organization	Non-adaptive	Slow	Responsive	Adaptive	Highly adaptive
Character	Extremely	Low	Flexible	High	Unquestionable

more urgent a fix becomes. Remember, it takes time to change an organization. That is why we spend so much time and effort in developing a profile of competitors' future behaviors.

Strategy

Strategy is a measure of the firm's creativeness and aggressiveness. As the competitive index goes up, so must the creative activities of the firm (known as research and development) as must its marketing aggressiveness. Reviewing Schumpeter's concept of creative destruction can help us understand what is going on. According to Schumpeter, environmental change is driven by the competitor's creativity in a given segment. For example, the computer processor manufacturer who is first able to deploy light processing technology will creatively destroy the value of the manufacturer who specializes in the current technology.

When we look at the competitive index, we can immediately understand the intensity of competitors' future creative destruction efforts in our competitive segment. If we do not match that level of effort, we will be eliminated. The same is true of marketing.

Organization

The next context-dependent area is organization. Areas like the CEO, the firm's leadership, culture, strategic planning, and others affect the ability of the firm to adapt. Clearly, certain types of CEO behaviors, leadership, and culture are well suited for a competitive context that involves slow change and low levels of competition (levels 1 and 2). It is equally clear that level 2 CEO behaviors, leadership, and culture will kill an organization that has moved into a level 4 or higher competitive index. For example, level 2 leadership (highly controlling, goal focused) will simply not work at level 4, where empowerment and individual creativity are critically important. The organizational measurements of Corporate IQ show the ability of the firm to adapt at appropriate levels. As the competitive context becomes more and more complex, the ability of the company to adapt becomes more important to profitability. Again, it all has to do with keeping the company in the profit zone.

Organizational Character

Organizational character is the driving force of sustainability. It is important to remember that character is the only area of the firm that is not context dependent. Level 5 is the only standard of behavior for smart companies. Smart companies value subordinates. I have talked a lot about corporate humility. Needless to say, unless corporate humility is a value, a company's leaders will generally become egocentric control freaks.

Ethics is another area of character that must be of the highest level. Regardless of the competitive index in which a firm is operating, any breach of ethics has the potential to destroy the firm. To validate that statement, one has only to look at the Enron fiasco.

In some ways, corporate character reflects a company's values, but in reality, it is much more. Corporate character is the bedrock that underlies all organizational activities. Corporate character not only fosters iconoclastic behavior, it also creates an internal and external atmosphere of uncompromising integrity that can impact every aspect of the company's life.

I have graphically portrayed a high level view of all of this below. Notice that the firm's competitive context is at level 4.0 and that strategy and organization must be able to operate at those levels to remain in the profit zone. Notice also that the standard for corporate character is 5.0.

THE 17 AREAS OF CORPORATE IQ

Figure 14.2 reveals the areas of the firm that fall under each of the three broad areas. Each of the 3 areas is further subdivided into 17 components.

To more effectively explain how the process works, I'll take one attribute of each of the three broad areas and demonstrate how to use this approach. Remember: the whole point is to keep the company in the profit zone, defined as "0.5 points of the competitive index." Let me show you how it works.

FIGURE 14.2   *The 17 Areas of Corporate IQ*

STRATEGY	ORGANIZATION	CHARACTER
Marketing	CEO attributes	Values
Innovation	Managers	Ethics
Product-technology	Culture	Value of people
Product portfolio	Formal structure	Excellence rating
	Intelligence systems	Quality and process
	Corporate strategy	
	Attitude toward change	
	Internal technology applications	

Strategy: Sales Aggressiveness

Notice in Figure 14.3 that I have presented a subset of the firm's marketing aggressiveness called "sales aggressiveness." Let us assume that the competitor index is 4.5.

Notice that the competitive index is around 4.4, but the dark dot that represents the current level of the firm's sales aggressiveness is around 2.9. Based on research, the difference between the company's sales aggressiveness and that of the firm's competitors (-1.5) will have a critical impact on the future profit of the company if not corrected. A simple way to understand the profit impact is as follows:

Difference = -0.5 or less   Impact = None (in the profit zone)
Difference = -0.51 to -1.0   Impact = Marginal
Difference = -1.1 to -1.49   Impact = Serious
Difference = -1.5 or more   Impact = Critical

The measurement of Corporate IQ is based on the differences cited above. The scale was changed to reflect more precise differences like -1.3 or -2.3. Otherwise, the principle is exactly the same.

The analysis indicates that the company is currently designed to compete with a sales strategy that is competitive but certainly not aggressive. A competitive strategy suggests that the firm attempts to keep pace with competitors. Notice that the appropriate sales aggressiveness at a competitive index of 4.4 is one of moderately high aggressiveness. Because the value is between 4.4 and 5.0, it will be necessary to move sales aggressiveness even closer to 5.0 or highly aggressive.

Some people look at the graphic and suggest that it might be difficult for a manager to understand. My experience has been just the opposite. Be-

FIGURE 14.3   *Marketing (Aggressiveness)*

Factor	Level 1	2	3	4	5
Sales aggressiveness	Low	Moderately low	Competitive	Moderately high	Highly aggressive

cause each industry segment is different, managers who are familiar with the segment have little trouble explaining what an aggressive level of sales is, or what a highly aggressive level of sales is. Defining each is rarely a problem.

For those who believe that this approach sacrifices some of the benefits of the traditional strategic management approach, such as "goal setting," I suggest that you rethink that view. Figure 14.4 presents all of the area called marketing aggressiveness. Notice that it clearly provides for goal setting in the area called market share. If you look at that area carefully, you will observe that, as the competitive index goes up, the company must set market share goals that reflect the future profit for the company. The higher the competitive index, the more aggressively the firm must seek to take market share from others.

Organization: Leadership Style

In the case of leadership style (a subset of Management), it appears that the firm's managers are moderately controlling (level 2.1). Again, the competitive index is 4.4, which leaves us with a difference of -2.3 (see Figure 14.5). That difference will have a critical impact on profit if not corrected.

I would like to point out the logic of this kind of thinking. In a competitive environment of level 4.4, high levels of uncertainty should be expected. Control-oriented managers (levels 1 or 2) will fail in this environment, because only moderate to high levels of empowerment will allow the firm to deal effectively with the numerous surprises that characterize the level 4.4 environment. This is not rocket science, just logic.

Character: Ethics

As I said earlier, organizational character is not context dependent. Only one level of character is acceptable: level 5. The character of the organization provides the stability required for internal adaptive capabilities as well as the behaviors that foster long-term customer relationships. In this particular example, I have considered the ethical standards of our fictitious company.

FIGURE 14.4   *Marketing (Aggressiveness)*

Factor	Level 1	2	3	4	5
Sales aggressiveness	Low	Moderately low	Competitive	Moderately high	Highly aggressive
PR/Advertising aggressiveness	Negligible	Moderate	Competitive	Aggressive	Highly aggressive
Market strategy	Maintain market	Maintain market	Grow with market	Expand market	Increase market share

Notice that the company has provided no clear-cut ethical policies. I am often astonished when I discover a company with one of those somewhat mystical ethical statements that contains a lot of words but very little content. Smart companies make ethics clear and understandable. Things like fraud, theft, discrimination, sexual harassment, and lying are simply not tolerated at smart companies. They put it into writing, and they put it into action.

In my interviews with the top ten smartest companies, I would often ask a question about what the company would do if a supervisor failed to promote a subordinate solely because of gender or racial prejudice. In every case, such behavior is clearly not tolerated. Let me be very clear about this. The difference between talking about an ethical standard and living that standard is summed up in one word: *consequences*. At smart companies, everyone knows that you walk the talk or you leave. *That* is how you define excellence.

ON BECOMING A SMART COMPANY

One of my objectives in writing this book was to avoid the highly technical approach that I sometimes see in other books. If a manager wants to apply the principles in this book, all they have to do is focus on Chapters 5 through 8, which deal with the various aspects of Corporate IQ.

FIGURE 14.5   *Management (Organizational)*

Factor	Level 1	2	3	4	5
Leadership style	Controlling	Moderately controlling	Results oriented	Empowering	Inspirational

FIGURE 14.6 *Ethics*

Policies	1 Non-existent	2 Hazy	3 Situational	4 Clear standards	5 Unquestionable standards

A word of caution: Be sure to use an outside organization to help you determine the future competitive context. In almost every study I have supervised or completed, internal managers consistently underestimate the level of the future competitive context by about 1.0 points. In fact, most of the time, they estimate it at level 3.0. The reason is somewhat complex. Basically, because most people resist change, they will often predict the future as highly predictable (level 3.0 or lower), simply because they do not want to deal with a lot of change and uncertainty.

Another caution has to do with who you poll to get some of your values. For example, I have seen a number of situations where senior executives thought that they were perceived as being level 4 or 5 leaders. Rather than being charismatic and highly empowering, their subordinates rated them as level 2 leaders, or highly controlling and risk-averse. The point is simply that you have to provide a way for the people being managed to answer some of these questions anonymously. Now that you understand the approach, it is time that you went ahead and conducted a Corporate IQ assessment of your own company.

THE CORPORATE IQ QUESTIONNAIRE

Part I: Competitive Context

Important. Be sure to answer based on what you expect the competitive segment to be in *three years*. Check the answer that best indicates your personal
understanding.

1. Which of the following best describes the marketing segment in which
   your organization is competing?

   A. A monopoly; No competition; Very slow change; Extremely predict-
      able.
   B. Extremely low level of competition; Slow change; Few competitors.
   C. Competitive but not too challenging; Fast change; Mostly predict-
      able.
   D. High levels of competition; Very fast change; Moderately unpredict-
      able.
   E. Overwhelming competition; Supersonic change; Almost totally un-
      predictable.

2. Which of the following best describes the level of competitor innovation
   you see in the segment?

   A. No innovation; Few or no new products.
   B. Little innovation; Occasional new products.
   C. Moderate levels of innovation; A steady pace of new products.
   D. A few breakthrough products; High levels of innovation; Frequent
      new products.
   E. Overwhelming innovation; Extremely high levels of new product in-
      troductions.

Part II: Corporate IQ Factors (The Organization)

Each of the following questions refers to your organization. Specifically, they refer to the part of your organization that competes in the segment described in Part I above. Again, please be sure you answer every question.

1. Which of the following best describes your firm's (organization's) approach to *marketing*?

    A. We are nonaggressive; We expect the customer to find us; No advertising or public relations strategy.

    B. We are slightly aggressive; We will respond to competitors if forced; Little or no advertising or public relations activities.

    C. We keep pace with competitors; We might be described as a "fast follower;" We match competitors sales, advertising, and public relations activities.

    D. We are aggressive; We like to be the first mover; Very proactive sales, advertising, and public relations activities.

    E. We get to the customer first; We are extremely aggressive first-movers; Highly aggressive sales, advertising, and public relations approach.

2. Which of the following best describes your firm's approach to *innovation* and the creation of new products and processes?

    A. Noninnovative.

    B. A follower approach; Benchmark others; Low level of innovation.

    C. A competitive innovator; Keep pace; Benchmark others; Little creativity within the organization.

    D. Very innovative; We seek new areas of product opportunity; A creative, innovative organization.

    E. Extremely innovative; We are out-of-the-box thinkers; We create the future.

3. Which of the following best describes your firm's approach to the *integration of technology* into its products and services?

    A. Little or no effort in this area.
    B. Minimal focus on integrating technology into products and services.
    C. We maintain balance with competitors; We keep pace with the competition.
    D. We stay ahead of the curve; We're adept at anticipating customer needs.
    E. We are the industry leader; We continually maintain first-mover advantage.

4. Which of the following best describes your organization's *product portfolio,* that is the balance of old (declining sales), mature (level sales), and new (high growth/high profit) products?

    A. Most of our products are in the mature or declining stage.
    B. Most of our products are in the mature stage; Level sales, but no high growth products.
    C. We maintain a balance of products; A few new products; Mostly mature products; A few declining products.
    D. We have a nice balance of new, high-growth products and mature, level-sales products.
    E. We have a lot of new, high-growth products with the balance being low-growth and mature products.

5. Which of the following best describes the *CEO* (or senior manager of the competitive segment)?

    A. Control oriented; A disciplinarian; Obsessed with the present and with performance; Little or no ability to value subordinates.
    B. Control oriented; Rewards those who maintain the status quo; Little or no ability to value subordinates.
    C. Objectives oriented; Moderately slow to change; Values performers and those who meet personal objectives.
    D. People oriented; Values subordinates; Sets a standard of excellence.
    E. Expects subordinates to value people; Values subordinates; Expects exceptional excellence and will help others achieve it; A great coach.

6. Which of the following best describes the *managers* in your organization?

    A. Strict disciplinarians; Results are all that matter; Highly controlling.
    B. Results oriented; Control oriented; Little or no value of people or subordinates.
    C. Performance oriented; Focus on results; Little value of people or subordinates.
    D. Coach, appreciate, value, and recognize subordinates; Credit others when a job is well done; Appreciate excellence in every area.
    E. The ultimate empowering coach; Love to see others do well and get recognized; Great at showing appreciation for others and recognizing their contributions.

7. Which of the following best describes your organizational *culture?*

    A. Don't rock the boat; Never share new ideas.
    B. Maintain the status quo; Do your job; Thinking is not your job.
    C. Maintain the status quo; Unquestioned obedience; Respond when asked.
    D. Challenge the status quo; Everyone has a part in our future.
    E. We terminate managers who do not value and listen to their subordinates; Everyone's job is to be a part of creating the future.

8. Which of the following best describes the *formal structure* of your firm?

    A. A steep hierarchy; Departmentalized bureaucracy.
    B. A hierarchy organized around functions; Bureaucracy.
    C. A divisional structure with separate product or geographical managers.
    D. A matrix or cross functional organization.
    E. A matrix structure that rewards those who cross formal lines of authority to get the job done.

9. Which of the following best describes how your organization gathers *information?*

   A. We get financial statements.
   B. We use computer analysis of sales, customers, etc.
   C. We get all of the above, plus have a business or competitive intelligence function.
   D. We have a global intelligence, information-gathering team with direct access to the CEO.
   E. All of the above plus; The intelligence function is highly valued by our entire organization (they have clout).

10. Which of the following best describes how your organization does *corporate strategy?*

   A. We do an annual budget.
   B. We do an annual budget plus a mission statement.
   C. We do a budget, a mission statement, and a SWOT analysis (strengths, weaknesses, opportunities, and threats).
   D. We create a strategic plan that is based on the future; Highly creative; Assumes nothing.
   E. We use multiple approaches that are highly creative; We assume nothing about the future, including "what business we will be in;" We design our strategy from the future back.

11. Which of the following best describes the ability of staff and senior managers to do creative strategic work (out-of-the-box thinking and creative problem solving)?

   A. Extremely low.
   B. Moderately low.
   C. A few.
   D. A moderately high percentage.
   E. A significant percentage.

12. Which of the following best describes your firm's *internal technology* (the internal technology systems that support operations) approach?

    A. Extremely slow; Far behind the curve.

    B. Slow; Add technologies and systems when forced to do it.

    C. As required to keep pace; Avoid adapting any technology too early.

    D. We constantly try to make sure we're anticipating the future technology needs of our organization and our customer.

    E. We have a total commitment to anticipating future technology requirements; We are a first-mover.

Part III: Corporate IQ (Organizational Character)

13. Which of the following describes your corporate attitude toward *product and process quality?*

    A. We don't concern ourselves with quality or our processes.

    B. Little concern for quality of processes.

    C. We have a formal total quality program that focuses on product quality and the processes used to handle and deliver products.

    D. Excellent quality and processes are the minimum at our organization. We have a formal measurement program.

    E. We expect excellence; quality is a way of life in our organization.

14. Which of the following best describes your *corporate values* (the standards and principles that guide decisions and actions)?

    A. We have values, but they're just not positive or people focused; It's all about doing what you have to do to get the job done . . . regardless.

    B. We don't have any focus on values; There are really no guidelines about how we treat others, our standards, etc.

    C. Our values are pretty standard; Do a good job and you'll keep it; We don't make managers accountable for how they manage others or how people relate to others.

    D. We have a clear set of values; We expect everyone to value others; We expect openness; We encourage people to stand up for doing the right thing.

    E. We are a principled, values-based organization; Everyone in our organization is accountable for how we treat customers, our peers, and our subordinates.

15. Which of the following best describes the *ethical standards and practices* at your firm?

   A. Little attention is paid to ethics; It's mostly an attitude of "avoid trouble" or not getting caught.
   B. We don't have a formal ethics statement but try to be honest.
   C. We have an ethics statement that says a lot of nice things; There are no real hard and fast standards, however.
   D. We have specific standards of ethical behavior; We provide employees with clear guidance when it comes to what we view as right or wrong.
   E. We have an ethical standard that clearly states what our organization views as absolutely right and wrong; We train all employees on our ethics; There is discipline, including termination in some cases, if our ethical standards are violated.

16. Which of the following best describes *how your organization values people?*

   A. People are discounted in our organization.
   B. People are necessary but unappreciated.
   C. Some people are valued, but it depends on who their manager is.
   D. Our managers are expected to value their subordinates and to communicate that value.
   E. Our managers are accountable for valuing their subordinates; They spend a great deal of time and expense to make sure people are recognized and valued.

17. Please respond to the following statement: "The firm is absolutely committed to exceptional excellence in the areas of products, customer relations, processes, and how every employee is valued, recognized, and treated."

   A. Strongly disagree.
   B. Disagree.
   C. The company really does not focus on this area.
   D. Agree.
   E. Strongly agree.

ADMINISTERING THE CORPORATE IQ ASSESSMENT

The competitive context is derived from questions 1 and 2. This is one of the most difficult aspects of computing Corporate IQ. The reason is that most internal managers will underestimate the context by as much as 1.0. This error can devastate a company. If the firm's managers incorrectly estimate the context at level 3.0 instead of 4.0, the impact on the firm's bottom line could be substantial. For that reason, it is acceptable to add at least 0.5 to whatever competitive context is derived from your computations. Here is how you compute competitive context.

Begin by administering the questionnaire to at least ten people in the organization. Obviously, for the context-related questions, knowledgeable outsiders can be extremely valuable. Once you have the questionnaire responses, convert the letter answers to numbers (A = 1; B = 2; C = 3; D = 4; E = 5). Use a spreadsheet to record the answers, then compute the mathematical average of each question. Average the results from questions 1 and 2. You should get a number like 3.6 or 4.7. Be sure to calculate the average to one decimal point, as shown.

Next, make the same calculations for each of the 17 questions about the organization. Again, it is critically important that 80 percent of the answers come from people down within the organization. For obvious reasons, every respondent must be absolutely certain of anonymity. Otherwise, the responses will be biased. It's a good idea to let a trusted outsider gather the completed questionnaires.

COMPUTING THE INDEX

Let us assume that you have computed a competitive index of 4.1. Assume that you have also averaged the responses from each of the 17 questions as shown in Figure 14.7.

FIGURE 14.7   *Competitive Index Computation*

The Competitive Segment: Competitive Index = 4.1

The Firm:	Raw Score	Difference	CIQ Index
Marketing aggressiveness	3.0	-1.1	6
Innovation aggressiveness	2.7	-1.4	5
Product technology	3.4	-0.7	8
Product portfolio	3.1	-1.0	7
CEO attributes	3.4	-0.7	8
Managers	2.5	-1.6	4
Culture	2.9	-1.2	6
Structure	3.4	-0.7	8
Decision systems	3.0	-1.1	6
Strategy	2.2	-1.9	3
Strategic capacity	4.0	-0.1	10
Internal technology applications	3.8	-0.3	9
Product quality/process	2.8	-1.3	6
Values	2.5	-1.6	4
Ethics	2.0	-2.1	2
Value of people	1.9	-2.2	2
Excellence	2.8	-1.3	5

CIQ Index Computation (based on difference between competitive index and the attribute):

-0 through -0.25	10 points (or 100%)
-0.26 through -0.50	9 points
-0.51 through -0.75	8 points
-0.76 through -1.0	7 points
-1.1 through -1.25	6 points
-1.26 through -1.50	5 points
-1.51 through -1.75	4 points
-1.76 through -2.0	3 points
More than -2.0 2 points	

CIQ Index Computation for Corporate Character (always use an index of 5.0):

Product quality and process

Values

Ethics

Value of people

Excellence

In the case of our subject above, the firm's Corporate IQ is 88. At best, that is a marginally low score. Based on my research, I would expect this company to have little success in the competitive environment. Go back and look at the company's scores in the area of Corporate Character. Those extremely low scores indicate that the company has little commitment to its people or to ethical behavior. This company is on its way out of business.

Again, it is important to remember that the 12 factors related to Strategy and Organization are always measured against the competitive context. At the same time, Corporate Character is always measured against an index of 5.0. A company's ethics, processes, quality, values, value of people, and commitment to excellence must always be of the highest standards if the firm is to achieve sustainable performance.

A FINAL COMMENT

You may remember the comment from the manager at Kingston Technology about when he came to work at the company: "I had to forget everything I'd learned in my MBA." I am sure by now that you have figured out that the entire approach of Corporate IQ is radically different from what is taught in most MBA programs.

The problem we have in business education today is a classic paradigm problem, much like the ones that Joel Barker has spent much of his time writing and talking about. The world has changed, but most in the academic field have not. Let me explain why I am saying that.

A lot of people in the field, such as best selling author Richard D'Aveni, are openly commenting on the outright inadequacy of the traditional, mission-vision approach to managing organizations. A lot of bestselling books are focusing on complexity and the need for organizations to forget about historic competencies and focus on what they need to become. "How has that impacted what is taught in most university business schools?" you might ask. The answer is simple: "Little or none."

Little if any research links the traditional approach to managing and corporate strategy to corporate performance. Let me say that again: there is simply no evidence to support the validity of the system. Conversely, the research that underlies the Corporate IQ approach is backed by over 30 years of research by H. Igor Ansoff and his associates. In many instances, that research accurately indicated future problems for organizations. No other approach can make claims of possessing the predictive power of this system.

I think the most compelling argument for Corporate IQ is that it simply makes sense. It makes sense to understand the competitive context that a company will face. It also makes sense to custom-design a company for its unique segment and context. Corporate IQ provides a road map that will allow a manager to design a company to match both the complexity as well as the rate of speed of the firm's emerging environment. That is why the approach works.

It makes sense to understand what a company's competitors will do, then to create or custom-build a company that is ideally suited for that specific competitive environment. Clearly, strategy and organization must follow context.

It is my personal hope that you have found this book helpful in your management endeavors. My calling is to teach, and I delight in seeing people have those wonderful moments of discovery. If I have managed to teach just a little in this book, I believe the effort will have been worthwhile.

CORPORATE IQ™

Stage 1 Research Results

January 6, 2003
Jim Underwood, DBA

OVERVIEW

The research focused on the study of 15 companies, most of which were publicly held, international organizations. The companies included a broad spectrum of industries, including telecommunications, transportation, consumer products, and technology. The objective of the research was to test the validity of an organizational profiling technique developed by the researcher called Corporate IQ. The results of the research are as follows:

- Companies with high IQs (above 140) will generally rank in the upper 20 percent in ROI (return on investment) ranking in their respective industry segment.
- Conversely, those with low IQs (90 or under) will tend to rank in the lower 20 percent of their industry segment.
- In spite of the relatively small sample size, the correlation between Corporate IQ and ROI ranking was extremely high.
- It is reasonable to conclude that Corporate IQ is an accurate predictor of organizational performance in the target population. That is, smart companies really do outperform their lower IQ industry counterparts.

THE RESULTS

The Stage I (15 companies) results indicate an extremely high correlation between Corporate IQ and ROI (return on investment) ranking in the firm's industry segment. Firms with a high Corporate IQ (scale of 0 to 170) consistently ranked in the top 20 percent of their segment, while low IQ firms consistently ranked in the bottom 20 percent of their segment. Further, the research calls into question both equilibrium theory-based approaches to corporate strategy[1] (core competencies, competitive advantage), as well as Darwinian-based (complex adaptive systems) approaches.[2]

$n = 15$; $r = 0.945$; $r2 = 0.893$; 95% Confidence Interval 0.987 – 0.839

THE INITIATIVE

The initiative is the result of over ten years of related research by the author that deals with complex environments and corporate profit. Approximately 40 percent of the proposed model or corporate aspects were based on previous research conducted by H. Igor Ansoff and his associates. Ansoff also based the concept of competitor profile on previous work.[3]

The Ansoff research measured eight organizational variables (now included in the Corporate IQ research). Ansoff and his associates tested the model (1,000 studies over a 20-year period) in almost every country in the free world and in every major industry group and confirmed the power of the concept. The Ansoff model confirmed that companies that match using his model had *ROIs of 100 percent to 300 percent higher* than those that did not match.

This research is a continuation and expansion of Ansoff's work. The past ten years have involved research surrounding other variables that may impact organizational performance.[4] The result is a 17-variable model that measures organizational behavior in a number of areas, including marketing, innovation, leadership, ethics, etc.

The need for such research is evident due to numerous problems[5] with competency-based views of the organization[6] as well as the questionable nature of the foundations of complexity-based views[7] such as complex adaptive systems. In addition to the numerous studies conducted by Ansoff and his associates, this researcher has supervised or conducted over 80 studies of *Fortune* 500 firms, which revealed the consistent predictive power of the model.

THE IMPORTANCE

The research reveals that corporate performance and sustainability have little to do with focusing on historic competencies or with self-organization. Rather, the research reveals that organizations must be managed as complex systems in which the organization and the firm's competitive environment must be balanced, or matched. Corporate IQ provides the complex model and measurements that account for performance and sustainability.

THE TARGET COMPANIES

The target companies were generally publicly traded, international companies. The Corporate IQ assessment was administered under agreement of confidentiality to individuals within the study organizations who would be expected to have a reasonable understanding of the firm's practices. Due to the extremely sensitive nature of the output, all respondents, with the exception of one, required confidentiality.

The research instrument was administered to a number of individuals within each firm. In some cases, there were over 40 respondents. In others, the number of respondents was small. In either case, the historic use of the assessment instrument has demonstrated that the selection of a knowledgeable respondent will consistently provide the same level of accuracy as would multiple respondents.

Corporate IQ is the trademarked property of Jim Underwood.

Chapter 1

1. Joseph A. Schumpeter, *Creative Destruction* (New York: Harper, 1975). First published in 1942.

2. Joseph A. Schumpeter, *Capitalism, Socialism, and Democracy* (New York: Harper, 1972).

3. Richard Foster and Sarah Kaplan, *Creative Destruction: Why Companies That Are Built to Last Underperform the Market—and How to Successfully Transform Them* (New York: Doubleday/Currency, 2001).

4. Evan M. Dudik, *Strategic Renaissance* (New York: Amacom, 2000).

5. John W. Sutherland, *Systems Analysis: Administration and Architecture* (New York: Van Nostrand, 1981).

Chapter 2

1. Charles R. Darwin, *Origin of Species,* 6th ed. (London: John Murray, 1972), 42.

2. Jonathan D. Sarfati, *Refuting Evolution* (Green Forest, Arkansas: Master Books, 1999).

3. Henry Mintzberg, *The Rise and Fall of Strategic Planning* (New York: The Free Press, 1994).

4. Ralph D. Stacey, *Managing the Unknowable* (San Francisco: Jossey-Bass, Inc., 1992).

5. James C. Collins and Jerry I. Porras, *Built to Last* (New York: Harper Business, 1994).

6. Joseph A. Schumpeter, *Capitalism, Socialism, and Democracy.*

7. W.R. Ashby, *Introduction to Cybernetics* (New York: John Wiley and Sons, 1956).

8. Ram Charan and Jerry Useem, "Why Companies Fail," *Fortune,* 27 May 2002.

9. Sydney Finkelstein, "7 Habits of Spectacularly Unsuccessful Executives," *Smart Company,* July 2003.

Chapter 3

1. *Corporate IQ* is the trademarked property of The Dallas Strategy Group, Inc., and Dr. Jim Underwood.

Chapter 4

1. Maria Halkias, "A Wholesale Debacle," *Dallas Morning News*, 26 August 2003.

2. "Kodak Announces a Reorganization," *Dallas Morning News*, 22 August 2003.

3. John W. Sutherland, *Systems Analysis: Administration and Architecture* (New York: Van Nostrand, 1981).

4. http://atheism.about.com/librar/glossary/general/bldef_fuzzylog ic.htm

5. H.I. Ansoff and Edward Donalson, *Implanting Strategic Management* (Hertfordshire, UK: Prentice Hall International, 1991).

6. Ansoff and Donalson, *Ibid.*

7. Igor Ansoff originated the two concepts of marketing turbulence and innovation turbulence. Both concepts as presented in this book are adaptations of his original work.

Chapter 5

1. H.I. Ansoff, et al., "Empirical Proof of a Paradigmic Theory of Strategic Success Behavior of Environment Serving Organizations," in *International Management Review*, ed. D.E. Hussey (New York: John Wiley and Sons, 1993).

2. Alfred DuPont Chandler, *The Visible Hand: The Managerial Revolution in American Business* (Cambridge, Massachusetts: Harvard University Press, 1977).

3. John W. Sutherland, *Systems Analysis: Administration and Architecture.*

Chapter 6

1. http://knowledge.wharton.upenn.edu/articles.fmf?catid=14&article id=867

2. H.I. Ansoff and Edward McDonnell, *Implanting Strategic Management* (Hertfordshire, U.K.: Prentice Hall International, 1990).

Chapter 7

1. "Rebuilding the Garage," *The Economist* 356 (8179): 59-60 (2000).

Chapter 8

1. "Continental CEO Won't Rest on His Laurels," *Houston Chronicle,* 28 December 2003.

Chapter 10

1. Peter Burrows, *Backfire* (New York: John Wiley and Sons, 2003).

Chapter 12

1. John Helyar, "The Only Company Wal-Mart Fears," *Fortune,* 23 November 2003.

2. Everett M. Rogers, *The Diffusion of Innovations* (New York: The Free Press, 1983).

Chapter 13

1. H.I. Ansoff. Lectures at Alliant International University, San Diego, California, 1991.

2. *Training Magazine,* pub. VNU Business Media Company.

Appendix

1. As supported by the work of Michael Porter and many in the academic community.

2. As supported by the work of Peter Senge, Meg Wheatley, and others.

3. H.I. Ansoff, et al., "Empirical Proof of a Paradigmic Theory of Strategic Success Behaviors of Environment Serving Organizations." *International Review of Strategic Management.* New York: John Wiley and Sons.

4. James D. Underwood, *Thriving in E-Chaos* (Rosedale, California: Prima Publishers, 2001).

5. Richard A. D'Aveni, *Hypercompetition* (New York: The Free Press, 1994).

6. M.D. Ryall, "When Competencies Are Not Core: Self-Confirming Theories and the Destruction of Firm Values." Bradley Policy Research Center, University of Rochester, 1998.

7. Jonathan Sarfati, *Refuting Evolution* (Green Forest, AR: Master Books, 1999).

S

Share the message!

Bulk discounts
Discounts start at only 10 copies and range from 30% to 55% off retail price based on quantity.

Custom publishing
Private label a cover with your organization's name and logo. Or, tailor information to your needs with a custom pamphlet that highlights specific chapters.

Ancillaries
Workshop outlines, videos, and other products are available on select titles.

Dynamic speakers
Engaging authors are available to share their expertise and insight at your event.

Call Dearborn Trade Special Sales at 1-800-621-9621, ext. 4444, or e-mail trade@dearborn.com.

Dearborn™
Trade Publishing
A **Kaplan Professional** Company